D0063128

IT'S NEVER TOO LATE

TO BE WHAT YOU

MIGHT HAVE BEEN

IT'S NEVER TOO LATE

TO BE WHAT YOU

MIGHT HAVE BEEN

by BJ Gallagher

coauthor of *A Peacock in the Land of Penguins*

VIVA
EDITIONS

Published in the United States by Viva Editions, an imprint of Cleis Press Inc., P.O. Box 14697, San Francisco, California 94114.

Printed in Canada.
Cover design: Scott Idleman
Text design: Frank Wiedemann
10 9 8 7 6 5 4 3 2 1

Library of Congress Cataloging-in-Publication Data

Gallagher, B. J. (Barbara J. Gallagher), 1949-
It's never too late to be what you might have been / B.J. Gallagher.
    p. cm.
  ISBN 978-1-57344-357-9 (pbk. : alk. paper)
1. Career changes. 2. Quality of life. 3. Happiness. I. Title.

HF5384.H378 2009
650.1--dc22

                                      2009004898

CONTENTS

For Sam Beasley
My wise coach,
My generous friend,
My practical go-to guy,
And my beloved teacher

It's never too late to become what you
might have been.

—*George Eliot (Mary Ann Evans)*

INTRODUCTION

Mary Ann Evans really lived the words she wrote. Living in Victorian England in the mid-1800s, she wrote under a male pen name, George Eliot, because she wanted her work to be taken seriously. At the time, women could publish freely under their own names, but they were seen merely as writers of silly romances. Mary Ann wanted her skill and talent to be recognized, so she did what she needed to do to fulfill her ambition as a serious novelist.

It wasn't too late for her, and it's not too late for you, either.

- What are your passions and talents?
- Do you have gifts to share with the world?
- Have you ever given up a dream in order to be more "practical" in making a living?
- Do you long to pick up that dream again?
- Do you worry that perhaps it's too late to become who you might have been?

I wrote this book to help you answer these questions. You only go around once in this life, so why not live a life you love? Start now. Live now. Love now. Laugh now. Give full expression to who you really are. Go for that deferred dream—whether it's a new career, a new love, a new sport, or making yourself wealthy.

You were put on this earth to be the best <u>YOU</u> that you can be. If you don't do it, nobody else can.

CHAPTER 1

IT'S NEVER TOO LATE TO MAKE YOUR DREAM COME TRUE

I think you have to take charge of your own life and
understand that you're either going to live somebody
else's dream or live your own dream.

—Wilma Mankiller,
first female chief of the Cherokee Nation

When I was a little girl I had dreams. I dreamed of being a naturalist, working for *National Geographic* and traveling the world writing stories about animals. I dreamed of getting married and having a wonderful wedding. I dreamed of living in California forever. I dreamed of being famous. I dreamed of doing work that helped others. I dreamed of being pretty, smart, funny, and well-liked.

I didn't stop dreaming when I grew up. I added some new dreams and let go of others. Much to my surprise, many of my childhood dreams have come true over the years—just not exactly in the way I had envisioned.

I don't work for *National Geographic*, but I do travel extensively, teaching workshops and giving keynote speeches. I don't write magazine articles about animals, but I do write books about them—one about a peacock in the land of penguins, and one about a three-legged cat. I did get married at a lovely ceremony, but the marriage didn't last. I did move to California in 1974, after having spent my childhood traveling the world with my military family. I may not be as famous as Oprah, but the hundreds of thousands of people who buy my books know who I am. I am clearly doing work that helps others—my speaking gigs and books. And although I felt insecure in my younger years, today I see that others *do* think I'm smart, funny, and pretty. As Sally Field famously said in her Academy Award acceptance speech, "You like me! You really, really like me!"

What a happy surprise to discover that my dreams have come true. I discovered that I had what I wanted all along—I was just the last person to realize it.

DOWNSHIFTING OUT
OF THE FAST LANE

The story of Laurie and Harvey Smith is the perfect opening tale for this chapter on living your dream. Many people aspire to life in the fast lane— a fabulous place to live, high-powered careers that pay well, cool parties to attend, and a weekend home at the beach. For the Smiths, living their dream evolved over time—and ended up in the slow lane. It's a story that affirms what you already know: *The best things in life aren't things.*

"Most people who work in New York City end up retiring to Florida or having a heart attack," Laurie Smith explained. "We didn't want to do either."

I cracked up. I don't live in New York, but I've been there often enough to know what she meant. The lifestyle is fast-paced, intense, and competitive, as well as exciting, interesting, and fun—easy to see how one might burn out.

"Harvey and I had married in our thirties. Harvey was a senior executive with a large textile company and I was an ad copywriter, working in advertising and promotion for magazines like *Sports Illustrated* and other publications. We lived the Manhattan lifestyle just like you see it in the movies. We had a great apartment with stunning views of the whole city. We had decided not to have children so we had plenty of income to enjoy the lifestyle.

"In 1992, we bought a home in the Hamptons. It was wonderful—we worked hard in the city all week, then retreated to the Hamptons for weekends and holidays."

"Sounds like heaven to me," I commented.

Laurie nodded. "It was, but one's notion of heaven can change over time, and mine did. I began to get restless. I also began to burn out. Harvey and I both had high-powered, high-intensity jobs, and over time, they take their toll."

"Trouble in paradise?"

"Yes," Laurie agreed. "We'd each been in our respective careers for about twenty years, but now we began to rethink what it was we wanted. Harvey had been with the same company for twenty-three years and he was only forty-six. He had started as a trainee and was now running a division for the largest textile converter in the country. If you've ever had a difficult boss or coworker, you know how stressful that can be."

Harvey added, "Laurie thought it was more important for us to be healthy and happy over any financial rewards we were earning. When we started talking about finding a new life adventure, most people were incredulous that we would even think about leaving New York.

"Our search began systematically with where we wanted to live. We looked at a map and began to consider options. First, we eliminated the states that weren't of interest: too cold, too hot, too small, too far from family, landlocked, little diversity, and so on. Through a process of elimination, we narrowed in on the Southeast. Then we started visiting cities and towns where we thought we might like to live."

"You both quit your jobs at the same time?"

"Yes," Harvey replied. "Up until then it was kind of like a plan, but giving notice made it very real. It's kind of like parasailing or a roller coaster—scary but exhilarating at the same time.

"I remember that I went to my bank in Manhattan to close my account. The branch president happened to be the one to help me that day. He asked me why I was closing my account. I told him that my wife and I were moving to North Carolina. 'Did you lose your job?' he asked. 'No,' I replied, 'I just quit.' This middle-aged banker in his pinstripe suit looked at me with a mixture of disbelief, envy, and admiration as he blurted out, 'You must have a really big pair of balls to do something like that!'"

"That's a New Yorker for you!" Laurie said with a laugh.

"People are an important part of what makes a city wonderful or terrible, and it was the people of Charlotte who made us want to move here," Harvey explained.

"I recall calling Laurie one day when I was down here in Charlotte and she was still in New York packing up. 'A fire engine came racing down the street today and people actually pulled over!' I told her."

"They don't do that in New York?"

"You could die waiting for an emergency vehicle in New York," Laurie said.

"We noticed lots of things like that about how people treat each other once we got outside New York," Laurie continued. "It was a collection of little things that we thought would add to our quality of life. For instance, on one of our visits to Charlotte we were in a restaurant having dinner; we had sat at the bar while waiting for our table. Partway into our meal, someone who worked for the restaurant approached our table and asked, 'Excuse me, but did you leave your purse at the bar?' My purse had been sitting there for half an hour and no one stole it!"

"That's remarkable!"

"Yes," Harvey agreed. "We also noticed how people at the supermarket would actually put their carts back instead of leaving them haphazardly in the parking lots. They said hello to you when they passed you on the street. They waved when you drove into the neighborhood. In Charlotte, if you ask someone the time, they will tell you. In New York, if you ask people the time, they won't stop, because they think you're going to rob them. Quality of life was our number one priority, and these little things told us that the quality we were seeking was here."

"What did you do once you moved here?"

"We gave ourselves two years to look at options," Laurie replied. "We finally bought into a new franchise—but the franchisor failed. It was very disappointing. Things weren't going quite as planned."

"I told Laurie that Bill Gates never hires anyone who hasn't experienced failures," Harvey interjected. "You learn more by failure than you do by success."

"What did you do after the franchise tanked?"

"We could have kept our part of the franchise going but Laurie wasn't enamored," Harvey replied. "So we were struggling with it. Then I saw an advertisement for a coaching program at the University of North Carolina in Charlotte. At that time, few people had heard of business coaching, or life coaching, but the more I learned about it, the more it resonated with me."

"And what did you do, Laurie, while your husband was going to school?"

"I was Harvey's first coaching guinea pig," she said, smiling. "He was learning how to help people discover their right livelihood, so I asked him to help me find mine."

"And I loved helping her, of course," Harvey added. "We started with her love of animals, something she didn't realize ran so deep.

"Shortly after we arrived here, Laurie became involved in dog rescue. One day, we pulled into a gas station and found a stray puppy running between the gas pumps. No one knew anything about her, so we cleaned her up, took her to the vet, and found her a good home within a couple of days. It just grew from there. Soon we were fostering and placing dogs regularly and working with other rescuers around the country."

"As a result, it seemed to make sense for me to explore dog professions," Laurie said. "I thought I might be a dog groomer—combining my love of dogs with my experience in cleaning them up and caring for them. I spent time in a few local salons and found I was ready to make the commitment.

"I researched grooming schools and decided the best one for me was a four-month, full-time program in Lexington, Kentucky. So at age fifty, I left my husband in Charlotte, took an apartment in Lexington, and became a student again. I was studying forty hours a week, and Harvey commuted to see me every couple of weeks.

"I was terrified. I'd been working as an advertising copywriter, using my brain for twenty-plus years. Now I was doing physical labor. Grooming is a whole lot more than a bath and blow dry. You are working on moving targets with scissors and blades. Dogs are scared and don't want to stand still. I developed a tremendous empathy for dogs when I realized that this grooming is not a fun experience for them. The school I went to helped me develop very high standards of safety and sanitation—which I later found out many groomers don't learn because they are self-taught or attend inferior training programs."

"What did you do when you finished your certification?"

"When I first returned to Charlotte, I worked for other groomers I respected, to further develop my skills. When I was ready to launch out on my own, I decided on a business model that would allow me to groom dogs in the most stress-free environment possible—their own homes. And I quickly found there were a lot of people who didn't want to leave their dogs at a salon all day. Or their dogs were too old, or too nervous, or they'd had a bad experience with a salon.

"I was going for a higher-end clientele, people who would pay a little more for in-home service. The nicest mall in town is in an area called SouthPark, so I called my business SouthBark. It was very well received, and by the end of the first year I was booked two months in advance!"

"That's very impressive."

Harvey nodded. "I work with lots of start-up businesses, and I can tell you that identifying a niche is a great way to focus and build your business. Laurie would come home every night exhausted and covered with dog hair—but with a big smile on her face."

"I was doing what I loved but it was taking a toll on my body," Laurie said. "I worked at it from October 2006 to January 2008 but finally had to give it up. That was really hard to do. I miss my clients, both the two-legged and especially the four-legged ones."

"So what are you doing now?"

"Well," Laurie replied, "Coach Harvey reminded me that I have other talents and skills, and that perhaps it was time to develop some new ones. He is a real proponent of ongoing professional development."

"All the while Laurie was grooming," Harvey said, "I was building my coaching business. I've got a client base of over four hundred businesses and individuals, so I could really use her help."

Laurie added, "Now he helps other people live their dreams. I jumped back into my copywriting and marketing role and rewrote his website. I help him with sales and marketing."

"We like to say that Laurie rescues dogs and I rescue people," Harvey quipped.

"Great way to describe it," I said, chuckling. "Now, I have one last question to ask before we finish: What advice would you give others who want to make their dreams come true?"

"I'd tell them that dreams come in all shapes and sizes," Laurie replied. "Yours doesn't have to be as dramatic as ours—quitting your job. Dreams are different for different people. And even with the same person, his or her dream probably changes over time."

"I agree," Harvey said, nodding. "And remember, it's a process. You don't have to do it all at once, especially if you are risk-averse. You can do it in small steps. Start taking courses or getting certifications. Go on informational interviews to meet people in your field of interest. Find out what it's really like. People love to talk about their expertise."

"That's all great advice," I said. "But let me ask you a follow-up question. The two of you had successful careers before you made this change. You'd made good money and socked enough away for the future. Do you have any advice for people who aren't in such a good position to make a change?"

Harvey chuckled. "Well, we didn't start off in a good financial position. I began my career as a New York City high school teacher. I loved it, but I didn't love being poor. So in the early nineteen-seventies, I made my first big career change. I started as low man on the totem pole in a new job in a field I knew nothing about.

"In some ways, it's almost easier to change if you *don't* have a lot of money, because you don't have much to lose—you're not invested to the same extent you are after twenty years."

Laurie added, "I would advise people not to make this kind of change without a buffer, without enough money to last them twelve months while they're getting started in their new line of work. Any entrepreneur knows that you have to have a cushion to support you while you're getting your business up and running."

"As you consider making a change to pursue your dream, there are some key questions you need to ask yourself," Harvey explained. "First, what does *success* look like for me? Second, what attitude do I need to adopt in order to achieve this success? Third, what knowledge and skills do I need to have? Fourth, who are the people I am going to surround myself with?

"You need a community of support: models, mentors, supporters, friends, family—a mastermind group. Consider hiring a coach. I often tell people that if we had hired a coach when we were first considering a change, we would have made better choices. I have a coach now, for sure."

"Something else to keep in mind," Laurie interjected. "It's a lot easier to make a career change if it's your choice. It's a lot harder adjustment if you get downsized or fired—then you're *forced* into a change that isn't your choosing."

"So the underlying message is that you either choose for yourself or run the risk of others choosing for you," I said.

"Yes, the underlying message is that we *have* choices," Laurie concluded. "It comes down to this: Imagine living your life knowing that you never even tried to achieve something that was in your heart or something that was meaningful to you. You'd not only be robbing yourself, you would be robbing others of all that you had to offer."

"And one last thought I'd like to add," Harvey said. "There is more than one way to be successful. In my early career as a teacher I learned that in every individual there is a magnificence. If only we would take the time to find that magnificence in ourselves."

*For more information about Harvey Smith's
business coaching, visit his website:
www.CarolinaBusinessCoach.com.*

The very least you can do in your life is to figure out what you hope for. And the most you can do is live inside that hope. Not admire it from a distance but live right in it, under its roof.

—*Barbara Kingsolver, novelist*

IT'S NEVER TOO LATE TO
DREAM...

DISCOVER new possibilities.
REENERGIZE yourself.
EMBRACE the adventure.
ASK for help.
MAKE THE MOST of your life!

One can never consent to creep when one feels the compulsion to soar.

—Helen Keller, first deaf/blind person to earn a college degree

Desire, ask, believe, receive.

—Stella Terrill Mann, inspirational speaker, author

YES, YOU *CAN* HAVE IT ALL

Lisa Daily has a great life—with husband, kids, AND a great career as an author, newspaper columnist, and dating coach. How did she do it? I asked her to share her recipe for success.

"How did you know that's my favorite quote?" she asked. "'It's never too late to be what you might have been.' I've got that quote pasted on my refrigerator; it's on my desk; I carry it in my wallet. I just love that quote! Those are the words that guide my life."

"Me, too," I replied. "But I've only adopted that quote recently. I had other favorite quotes in years past. Tell me how 'It's never too late' has played out in your life so far."

"Well, I had a great role model in my mother," Lisa began. "In her early forties she went back to school. Prior to that, she worked in a dermatologist's office in Denver, where I grew up. She was the office manager, which was perfect for a young mom raising kids. She got off work at a reasonable hour and had Wednesdays off—golf day for doctors. But she'd always loved kids and wanted to work with young ones, so when my brother and I were teenagers, she went back to school to study early childhood education. She was working toward her degree, and a friend told her about a job as director for Catholic Charities' Child Development Center. On paper, she was certainly not the most experienced candidate, but she wanted that job—it was her dream job. She was on fire about making a difference in the lives of children. She got the job, of course. Once she made the decision to follow her passion, a lot of opportunities just opened up for her. She just recently retired, after twenty years working there."

"That's a great story. Tell me more."

"When I went to college, I got my degree in communications," Lisa continued. "After graduating, I worked in advertising as a copywriter. I loved it—working with brilliant, creative, talented people, traveling all over the place to shoot commercials, and thriving on the excitement, challenge, and constant stimulation.

"But when I was thirty, I gave birth to my son, and found that my priorities began to change. I hated the idea of being away from my baby so much of the time. I had been working seventy hours a week, traveling for stretches at a time, and that just wasn't going to work for me as a new mother.

"When my son was just two weeks old, we moved to Bloomington, Indiana, where my husband was going to attend grad school for the next two years. I knew that I had to continue working to help support our young family, but I didn't want the same schedule I'd been working prior to that.

"Fortunately for me, advertising agencies in Bloomington had a hard time finding good copywriters. So when I was offered a job, I had some leverage, though I didn't really realize that until later. All I knew at the time was that things had to be different. I told my prospective employer that I could only be in the office for two hours a day, from 8:30 to 10:30 A.M., and the rest of the day I would work at home. I also told them they had to match my former salary. Shockingly, they said yes."

"Wow, that's pretty remarkable."

"Yes, in retrospect I see how amazing that was," Lisa agreed. "All I can tell you is that having a new baby made me much braver than I ever would have been before. I knew what I wanted, what was important to me, and I just had to ask for it. Necessity gave me courage."

"That's great."

Lisa continued her story. "In those next two years, I got used to working at home. I loved the flexibility. I was able to do justice to both my work and my son, while my husband pursued his grad studies. It worked out perfectly for all of us.

"It was a smaller ad agency than I had worked for previously, and the work wasn't as interesting. The clients were kind of boring, and it seemed I just did the same thing month after month. But it was only for two years, so that was OK.

"When my husband finished his degree, he took a big corporate job in Minneapolis. He made plenty of money, so for the first time in my life, I didn't have to work. But I knew I still wanted to do *something*. I know myself well—I'm ambitious, creative, and thrive on challenge. I wanted some kind of career excitement, in addition to the challenge of being a good mom."

"So, what did you do?"

"My whole life, I've known two things about myself. First, I wanted to write a book; I've always known that sooner or later I would write a book. Second, I know that whenever I am around other people, somehow the conversation always seems to come around to love and romance, and they end up telling me their dating and relationship troubles. I'm not sure why that is; my mom seems to have the same effect on people. Maybe it's because I care about people—I want everyone to be matched up and happy.

"But I'm also a practical person. I can see the mistakes people make when they're dating and I seem to have a knack for coaching them on how to avoid or correct their mistakes. Over the years, I've often found myself coaching my friends—and even people I'd just met—about their relationships. Very often, they would say, 'Lisa, you should write a dating book.'

"I recall one friend in particular—her name is Tina. She was a dating train wreck! She needed advice but wouldn't take it from friends. She also read a lot of advice books. I remember thinking, *I want to write a book to help women like Tina.*"

"And so you did it."

"Yes," Lisa said. "Becoming an author was the perfect next step for me. I get to stay home with my kids—I now have two youngsters. I take my laptop down to the beach a couple of days a week to work, and I can't imagine any work that is more challenging, thrilling, or fulfilling than what I get to do every single day.

"I didn't know anything about publishing; I didn't know anyone who was an author. But I'm really a researcher at heart and I knew I could do it. I relied on my own experience a lot. I was a good dater and married a great guy, so I could speak from experience. I also had great women in my family and I drew on their experience as well. My aunt was a smart, insightful woman who was happily married for fifty years to my uncle. So I could learn from her and others in my family. That was a blessing.

"I originally decided to self-publish my book and came up with a catchy name—*Stop Getting Dumped,* which was picked up a few months later by a major publisher. On the surface, it's a dating advice book. But it's really a chocolate-covered empowerment book. It's about asking for what you want, knowing that you deserve it—being brave and putting your heart out there."

"Love it," I said, smiling at Lisa.

"Well, I don't just write about it, I live it." Lisa said. "I check in with myself every so often and ask, *Does my life look the way I want it to look? More important, do I feel the way I want to feel?*"

"What advice do you have for others who want to find their dream job, attract a dream relationship, build a dream lifestyle?"

Lisa thought for a moment before replying. "Well, I guess that brings

me back full circle to the beginning of our conversation and that quote we both love so much: It's never too late to be what you might have been. I'd tell people to be fearless—to ask for what you want, to go after the life or the job or the dream you've always wanted.

"I hear people say 'I'd love to write a book, but only one in a hundred and seventy-five thousand manuscripts ever gets published, so I'd probably be wasting my time.' Or 'I'd love to start my own business, but the chances of making any real money are only one in ten thousand.'

"So many people are paralyzed by their fears that they never get started with that first step. When I hear that there's only a one in a million chance of success at something, I think, *Well, somebody is going to be the one, and it might as well be me.* That's what I would say to anyone who is hesitating or fearful or just shy about following their dream, or about changing their life in a significant way. Somebody's going to be the one—it might as well be you."

Lisa Daily is the author of *Stop Getting Dumped.*
She recently achieved her lifelong dream of writing a novel,
Fifteen Minutes of Shame. Her new book is
How to Date Like a Grown-up.
For more about Lisa, visit her website: www.lisadaily.com.

There are people who put their dreams in a little box and say, "Yes, I've got dreams, of course I've got dreams." Then they put the box away and bring it out once in a while to look in it, and yep, they're still there. These are great dreams, but they never even get out of the box. It takes an uncommon amount of guts to put your dreams on the line, to hold them up and say, "How good or how bad am I?" That's where courage comes in.

—*Erma Bombeck, newspaper columnist, humorist, and author*

CALIFORNIA DREAMIN'

Arnold Schwarzenegger has spent his whole life living his dreams, one after another. As a young, unknown bodybuilder in Austria, he had big dreams. He knew his destiny was in America, not Europe, and he often credits his dreams with enabling him to survive a harsh childhood. His father, a policeman, was a brutal disciplinarian. As he told *Fortune* magazine in 2004, "My hair was pulled. I was hit with belts. So was the kid next door. It was just the way it was. Many of the children I've seen were broken by their parents, which was the German-Austrian mentality....It was all about conforming. I was the one who did not conform, and whose will could not be broken. Therefore, I became a rebel. Every time I got hit, and every time someone said, 'You can't do this,' I said, 'This is not going to be for much longer, because I'm going to move out of here. I want to be rich. I want to be somebody.'"

Schwarzenegger's first dream was to become the greatest bodybuilder in the world—Mr. Olympia. In 1970, at age 23, he became the youngest man to win the title, an honor he still holds today.

His second goal was to become a movie star—a bit of a challenge considering his thick German accent. "It was very difficult for me in the beginning—I was told by agents and casting people that my body was 'too weird,' that I had a funny accent, that my name was too long. You name it, and they told me I had to change it. Basically, everywhere I turned, I was told that I had no chance." ("Ask Arnold," www.Schwarzenegger.com.)

After a few less-than-notable films and performances, Schwarzenegger finally achieved some recognition with his 1977 bodybuilder film, *Pumping Iron*. But his big break didn't come until 1982, with the box-office hit *Conan the Barbarian*. The '80s saw a series of successes for the ambitious young Austrian, including his signature 1984 hit, *The Terminator*. The public appetite for action films was at its peak and he, along with Sylvester Stallone, became an action hero superstar.

The year 1990 brought Schwarzenegger's first taste of political life, when he was appointed chairman of the President's Council on Physical Fitness. After holding that appointment for three years, until 1993, he gained attention for his work with the American Red Cross. People speculated about a political future for the bodybuilder-turned-action-hero. In an interview with *Talk* magazine in 1999, Schwarzenegger was asked if he thought of running for office. He replied, "I think about it many times. The possibility is there, because I feel it inside."

The rest, of course, is history. In 2003, on *The Tonight Show* with Jay Leno, Schwarzenegger announced his candidacy for governor of California in the recall election for Governor Gray Davis. He won by over a million votes. This 56-year-old Austrian immigrant launched his third career, continuing to live out his dreams.

Is it too late for you to live YOUR dreams? Just ask California's Governator.

FINDING THE WRITE WAY

Sue Voyles is a communicator. She makes her living as a wordsmith, doing what she loves to do. Hers is an interesting journey with many twists and turns, ups and downs.

"I always knew I'd be a writer," Sue began her story. "Growing up, I loved to read and regularly visited the library. Then, when I was going to high school in the seventies, Watergate dominated the news, Woodward and Bernstein became household names, and journalism was perceived as an exciting career.

"I spent my first year of college at a small liberal arts school in Illinois, where I excelled in English and worked on the student newspaper. Then I transferred to Wayne State University in my home state of Michigan—that's where the legendary reporter Helen Thomas got her journalism training. Many years later I had the opportunity to meet her and it was such a thrill."

"So, did you get your degree in journalism?" I asked.

"Yes," Sue replied. "I left college for a while and then went back to school, this time at Madonna University, a small Catholic school in Michigan. I was twenty-eight when I finally finished my BA in English and journalism. One of my professors there, Sister Jacqueline, was especially influential in my education and in my career, too. After graduation in 1986, I was offered a job in the university's PR and fund-raising department, so I stayed on campus for another two years."

"Trouble leaving the academic nest?" I teased.

Sue chuckled. "You might say that. In fact, I came back to higher education again later on. I've always loved learning, education, and academic environments. Writing and teaching are my two natural gifts, so I'm quite happy in a college or university. But I didn't stay there forever. I left and went to work for the Detroit Institute of Arts—in membership, though I would have preferred to work in public relations.

"I got my wish eighteen months later, when I was offered a job in PR at Family Services Inc. in Detroit, a United Way agency. A friend of mine was in their development office doing fund-raising and she was instrumental in bringing me on board. She knew how I loved communications of all types and thought I'd be a good fit for the PR job and the organization. She was right. I stayed there seven years and loved it. When you work for a small organization, you're very often a one-person department so you have to do it all—press releases, publications, event planning, and more. I thrived on the variety and stimulation."

"Why would you ever leave a job that was such a perfect fit for you?"

"Ah, well, there are other facets of life that have their influence on career decisions and job choices," Sue replied. "In 1996, I was home on maternity leave after the birth of my second child, when my old boss at Madonna University called and offered me a job in marketing. I recall talking it over with a friend of mine, who said, 'Take it. You've got a toddler and an infant; the job is only five miles from your home, instead of the thirty miles you're now commuting; it's a smart move.' So I accepted the new job."

"How did that work out?"

"It was fine for a few years," Sue continued. "I was marketing their academic programs and enjoying being back on campus again. Then, in July 1999, my husband lost his job. He was also a communicator and had started his career as a newspaper reporter. So we set up a business together—sort of a fallback for him while he looked for another job.

We registered our DBA [doing business as] and got the ball rolling. In September of 1999, we got our first client, a local bank. We were going to do employee communications for them."

"So you were officially in business."

"Yes, and it felt really good. By this point in my career, I had developed a great network of professional contacts over the years. I've always been a natural at networking—joining and becoming active in professional organizations. I knew tons of people, especially in the nonprofit world. So I took to marketing our new business like a duck takes to water.

"In October, my husband landed another job, and we had to decide what to do with our little fledgling business. I thought about it for a while and really felt I could be successful with it. In January 2000 I told my husband that I wanted to give it a shot—I would give it one year, and if I wasn't making it by then, I would go get another job."

"That must have been exciting."

"It was," Sue replied. "But it also seemed like a practical decision. I had two young kids—a daughter in grade school and a son in preschool. It took enormous energy to handle the logistics of childcare and a full-time job. I wanted more flexibility and I wanted more quality of life balance."

"I'm sure millions of women feel exactly the same way."

"I'm sure you're right," Sue agreed. "In fact, I'm really proud that some of my part-time staff are women with small children who are also seeking work–life balance. I'm lucky that I found a way to get what I wanted. On my last day at Madonna University—in February—I got a call from my friend Michelle telling me that she had just landed the grant she'd been hoping for. 'Are you available to work?' she asked. So she became my second client. I was so excited when I got that phone call. Everything was falling into place.

"In June I landed some employee communications work with a business unit of General Motors. By December, the end of my first year of full-time entrepreneurship, I was convinced I could make a go of it. My family balance was good. I was happy."

"Don't you just love happy endings?"

"You bet! I was forty-one when I started that business, with only five hundred dollars in start-up capital, a PC, an Internet connection, and my Rolodex. Now, ten years later, I'm fifty years old and living my dream!"

"What advice would you give others who want to live their dreams?"

"I'd give them the same advice that Sandy Burgess, my friend from the Association for Women in Communication, gave me:

1. Keep your business and personal lives separate. Set up a business checking account separate from your personal account; get a business phone line; have a work area separate from your living area.
2. Use your network to get business.
3. Use your network to get help.

"The central question is: Are you running a business or sustaining a hobby? If you're running a business, you need to treat it like a business—keep business hours, get business cards printed, put up a website. You want clients to take you seriously, and it starts by taking your business seriously."

"Good, practical advice."

"I would also say that if you have the passion and commitment to succeed, it's never too late. I think I was a natural entrepreneur all along, but didn't know it until starting this business.

"While my husband was going through his job search in 1999, I was reading a book titled *Do What You Love, the Money Will Follow* by Marsha Sinetar. That book really encouraged me to take that first step into business. If you really love what you do, you won't mind getting up and going to the office in the morning. If you really love what you do, you won't mind networking and making sales calls. If you really love what you do, you won't find working hard. It's true—if you do what you love, the money *will* follow."

"Any other advice?"

"Be careful you don't put all your eggs in one basket. Don't become too reliant on one customer or client. Life is full of unexpected changes and if you don't diversify your business, you can get the rug pulled out from under you by one major client. My business kept going after 9/11 while some other businesses didn't. That's because I had a variety of clients.

"Also, don't be afraid to say no to an opportunity if it's not the right opportunity for you. I learned this the hard way. In the beginning, you say yes to everything because you need the business. But later on, I made a couple of mistakes by not picking up on cues that would have told me, This client is not a good fit for me. Over time, you have to learn to say no.

"And at the same time, be careful not to say no too quickly—to opportunities that might seem a little off-track but that might lead to something really wonderful. For instance, in 2002 I was asked to develop an online journalism course for the local community college. I wasn't sure at first, but I said yes because I loved journalism and it was a chance to share my passion with students. Now I teach that class one semester a year and I love it.

"Another terrific opportunity came my way because I always keep my eyes and ears open. In 2005, I heard via my professional network about a business magazine that might be for sale. I passed the information on to my client, who was interested enough to acquire the magazine in early 2006. The best part is that now I am the magazine's editor—working in journalism, which I love.

"If you learn from your experiences, and ask smart people for advice, you'll get good at knowing when to say no and when to say yes."

For more about Sue Voyles's writing, public relations,
and marketing, visit her website:
www.logos-communications.com.

Man, alone, has the power to transform his thoughts into physical reality; man, alone, can dream and make his dreams come true.

—Napoleon Hill, author of *Think and Grow Rich*

NEVER-TOO-LATE TIPS FOR
MAKING YOUR DREAM COME TRUE:

1.
Create a mental picture of what your life would look like if you were living your dream. The mind thinks in pictures, so make a "mental movie" of your dream come true. Play and replay this movie often.

2.
Manage your motivation. Read books; watch DVDs; listen to CDs that help keep your enthusiasm, energy, and commitment high.

3.
Keep your eyes and ears open. Opportunity is everywhere, if you're alert enough to recognize it.

4.
Practice active gratitude. Take a few minutes each day to notice the things in your life that you're grateful for—the place you live, your car, your pets, treasured possessions, friends, your job, etc. Appreciation of what you have brings more good things into your life.

5.
Ask for what you want. You might be surprised how often you can get it.

CHAPTER 2

IT'S NEVER TOO LATE TO START A NEW CAREER

To find a career to which you are adapted by nature, and then to work hard at it, is about as near to a formula for success and happiness as the world provides. One of the fortunate aspects of this formula is that, granted the right career has been found, the hard work takes care of itself. Then hard work is not hard work at all.

—*Mark Sullivan, author*

I come from a long line of late bloomers. My dad started college at UCLA when he was just 16, having skipped a couple of grades as a bright kid. He didn't do well that first year at the university, so he dropped out, enlisted in the military, and went off to fight in WWII. When the war was over, he used the GI Bill to go back to UCLA. This time he earned top grades, took on leadership roles in student government, and became president of his fraternity.

After graduation, he did a stint teaching ROTC, only to discover that he really didn't like teaching. Then he took a job selling Arrow shirts, in which he learned that sales wasn't for him. He finally reenlisted in the Air Force, where he served for the next 30 years.

Upon retirement, he was still relatively young, in his early 50s, so he began a second career as a banker, working for Bank of America for the next 10 years. Now retired from both the Air Force and the bank, he's worked as a census taker and later as a travel agent, to keep his mind and body active. At age 85, Dad is still going strong.

My own careers have been even more varied than my father's. My first jobs were in restaurants and bars, as a carhop, waitress, or barmaid. Then I moved up to clerical jobs—filing, answering phones, and general office duties. In college, I took on research jobs and teaching assistant positions.

I stayed in college and graduate school as long as I could—until I was 30, when I took my first "real job." I spent seven years on staff at the university, finding my way into the field of adult education and training, which I loved.

When it came time to try my wings outside the academic nest, I flew to a large metropolitan newspaper, where I was the manager of training and development.

As the newspaper business changed, so did I. I left the world of "real jobs" in 1991 and became self-employed—not something I was ever prepared to do. It's been a challenge to fly solo, without the support of a large organization around me. But it's also been exhilarating and affirming.

Since starting my own business, my passion has shifted from teaching seminars to writing books. My goal is to reach millions of people, earning a fabulous living, working from home in my jammies.

Is there another career change in my future? Who knows? After all, I am my father's daughter.

A WOMAN WITH A MISSION

Belinda Rachman was a special education teacher in New York for many years, working with severely emotionally disturbed young people—in schools and in mental institutions. It was hard work, but she felt called to help those who needed her. In her late 30s, she and her husband moved to Southern California, where Belinda got a job teaching special education in Vista (San Diego County).

During the performance review at the end of her first year, the school principal asked, "Who do you work for?"

"I work for the kids and their parents," Belinda answered.

"Wrong answer," the principal told her. "You work for the Vista Unified School District, and we didn't hire you to be a child advocate. You won't be getting tenure next year."

That conversation felt like a slap in the face. Belinda went home, called her mother, told her what happened, and said, "I want to go to law school."

"Go," her mother replied. "I'll pay."

Belinda explained the generous offer: "My mother had been a teacher in her early career and then went to law school when she was in her late 30s. I recall her studying for the bar exam and how hard it was. She made the decision to go back to school at a point when she was twenty years older than the other law students. And here I was—on the verge of doing the same thing. But oddly, I didn't really want to be a lawyer."

"Then why did you choose law school?" I asked.

"I think it was triggered by the conversation I'd had that day with my principal," Belinda replied. "He used the term *child advocate*. And law school somehow seemed familiar because I'd seen my mother do it. It didn't look like much fun, but it was familiar."

"What happened next?"

"I spent the next three years in law school. I was fortunate in that my husband could support me so I could focus solely on my studies. But I still wasn't thinking about becoming a lawyer. I didn't take any of those classes that teach you how to run a law practice. Instead, I was the editor of the law school newspaper and organized the student talent show. I did all the fun stuff. Finally, after my studies, I did take one class on how to pass the bar exam. I had decided that I might as well try to pass, even though half of all law students fail the bar the first time.

"I'll never forget those three days in the basement of the Pasadena Convention Center. While hundreds of us were downstairs sweating over the bar, the Dalai Lama was upstairs conducting teachings. It was an odd experience—as if his feet were walking around on the tops of our heads. It was a very peaceful three days—which is not normal for a bar exam. No one threw up; no fights broke out; no one cried; it was peaceful and serene. When I walked out of there at the end of the third day, I knew I had passed."

"So, then what?"

"Well, I had this law degree," Belinda continued, "and I felt an obligation to use it. I thought about my skill set—working with disturbed, crazy people. Where are they? I asked myself. In divorce court.

"My mom told me not to go there. She said, 'You'll hate it. People in divorce court are angry, mean, vindictive, and nasty. It's the worst kind of environment.'

"But I wanted to go where I could make the most difference, and I thought divorce court would be it. My teacher skills would stand me in good stead.

"My husband continued to support me so I didn't have to make money. I volunteered to do divorces for poor people—for $350 I would handle their divorces. My clients were strippers, welfare mothers, and even a runaway Mormon wife who had been smuggled out of a polygamous cult by an underground group. I never took a case I didn't believe in."

"It must have been very rewarding."

"Yes, it was," Belinda said. "But after eight years, I saw what a racket divorce is in California."

"Racket?"

"In California, divorce attorneys are the only attorneys with a law that protects their fees by the equity in their clients' homes," she explained. "So they drag things out as long as they can, filing all sorts of motions, stoking the emotional fires of their clients, stirring up as much adversarial drama as possible."

"That sounds like a terrible conflict of interest built into the system," I said.

She nodded. "You bet. Now I understood what my mother had warned me about. So after eight years, I decided I would do only divorce mediation. I'd already been doing it with a lot of my poor clients, anyway. I was often the only attorney handling their divorces—ending up working with both husband and wife, helping them negotiate the details of their breakup. They never had any property to fight over, so it was almost always about custody and visitation. That's exactly where you don't want to be adversarial—for the kids' sake.

"That was five years ago and I'm happy to report that it's worked really well. Most mediators have a success rate of about eighty percent, but mine is a hundred percent. It's not the lawyer in me who's doing it—it's the teacher.

"Everything I did in the past has served me well in my role as a mediator. I have a very powerful intention to find each person's bottom line and then find a solution that works for everyone.

"Word of mouth has brought me many affluent clients—military people from nearby Camp Pendleton as well as really rich people from Rancho Santa Fe. My flat fee rate of twenty-five hundred dollars is a bargain compared to the tens of thousands of dollars charged by most divorce attorneys. And it's a fine rate of pay from my perspective: I never have to go to court, it only takes me five to seven hours to handle most mediations—clients have to do some preparation work on their own—and I love the helpful contribution I'm making to these couples and families."

"What about the poor people whose cases you used to handle?"

"Oh, I still work with poor people, too," Belinda replied. "My rich clients subsidize my work with poor people. And I feel especially good because I'm taking money from the 'enemy'—those sharks who bring out the worst in their clients to drive their legal bills up. Those guys are dinosaurs. I hope that the work I do—it's called the peaceful divorce movement—is the harbinger of good things to come."

"What advice would you give people who want to go back to school or change careers?"

"When you do the work you love, you're happy," Belinda said. "I love my work and I love to get up in the morning. I didn't feel like that twenty years ago when I was working with severely disturbed kids in Harlem. In those days, I had to drag myself out of bed, drag myself to the train, dreading what I knew waited for me at the other end of the line.

"The other thing I'd say is that the skills, talents, and abilities you've developed in the past will probably be useful to you in whatever you're going to do in the future. I do believe that everything we do is a stepping stone to whatever's next. For instance, being a special ed teacher seems like it has nothing to do with being an attorney; but if you look deeper, you see that they both use the same skill set, working with people in emotional distress. So it's likely that past experiences have trained you perfectly for the future."

For Californians who seek a peaceful divorce,
take a look at Belinda's top tips for avoiding court at
www.divorce-inaday.com.

What is the recipe for successful
achievement? To my mind there
are just four essential ingredients:
choose a career you love, give it
the best there is in you, seize your
opportunities, and be a member
of the team.

—*Benjamin Fairless,*
CEO of US Steel

Think not of yourself as the architect of
your career, but as the sculptor. Expect
to have to do a lot of hard hammering
and chiseling and scraping
and polishing.

—*B. C. Forbes,*
founder of Forbes *magazine*

IT'S NEVER TOO LATE TO
LOOK FOR A
NEW CAREER...

CREATE your ideal job.

ARRANGE your life accordingly.

REHEARSE new roles.

EXPAND your repertoire of skills.

ENLARGE your professional network.

REMEMBER that today is all any of us have.

Sometimes you wonder how you got on this mountain.
But sometimes you wonder, How will I get off?

—Joan Manley, *author*

WHEN YOUR PASSION CHANGES

For some people, the dream job isn't so dreamy after a while. Frank Graff's story is that of someone who followed his passion for many years, only to find his passion shifted over time.

"When you were a kid, what did you want to be when you grew up?" I asked Frank.

"I wanted to be an astronaut," he replied. "That is, until seventh grade, when I had to get glasses. I remember walking out of the optometrist's office and saying, 'Hey, there are leaves on the trees!' Before getting glasses, the trees had just been big blobs of green on top of brown trunks. But in that moment, I also realized that my career hopes were dashed. You can't be an astronaut if you have to wear glasses. I could now see clearly what was on earth but I wasn't ever going to see what was in space."

"Oh, what a bittersweet story," I said. "What did you do next?"

"Well, I had always loved the news," Frank replied. "Every evening our family gathered at the dinner table to share our evening meal and watch the news on TV. Walter Cronkite was my hero. News in those days was really good—it was really a form of storytelling. I was enthralled with the stories: political stories, sports stories, tragedies, morality tales, and much more. I ate it all up.

"I was lucky that my high school in Toledo, Ohio, had a small closed-circuit TV station. We produced a half-hour news show once a week, broadcasting it to all the classrooms in the school. We did goofy little stories, but it was great hands-on learning.

"When I graduated, I went on to Ohio University, where they had a PBS station. There we produced a half-hour news show every night. Usually, only juniors and seniors got to anchor the news—rotating every two weeks. But I was talented and lucky—I was one of the first sophomores to do it. It was a wonderful experience and especially useful, since I was pursuing a degree in broadcast journalism.

"My junior year, I landed an internship in the Washington bureau of CNN. I was assigned to work with Charles Bierbauer, who was covering the Pentagon. He's a superb newsman whom I admired enormously. We still keep in touch. Imagine the thrill of walking into the Pentagon with him, getting my press pass, and then walking into the media section of the building and getting introduced to all these people I'd watched on TV during all those family meals. I was hooked!"

"What did you do when you graduated?"

"Another bit of luck," Frank replied. "It was 1982 and all-news TV was in its infancy. Because of the internship, I landed a job at CNN, which was just beginning, in Atlanta. I worked there for about three months and then one of my professors called me from Ohio University. 'I've got an assistantship in political science,' he told me. 'Do you want to come back and go to grad school?'

"So I did. All my friends, and my girlfriend, were still in Ohio, so I was eager to go back. I spent a year earning my MA.

"After grad school I got a job at a small station in northern Maine. It was 1983—I was twenty-three-years old and the morning anchor. You may not know this, but the United States is divided into two hundred and eleven TV markets, and they are ranked according to size. That little station in Maine was number two hundred and one, pretty close to the bottom. I remember telling Charles Bierbauer about my new job, and he quipped, 'Well, Frank, there's no place to go but up.' We both laughed about that.

"I spent a year and a half there, and it was quite an adjustment. I was a city kid now living in the wilds of northern Maine, where the snowfall each year was about a hundred and ten inches. Basically, it started snowing around Halloween and winter lasted until Easter. I had come from Ohio, where football is king, and as I drove around Maine to get the lay of the land, I noticed there were NO football stadiums anywhere. I learned that the local kids get a couple of weeks off from school in the fall to help with the potato harvest, then they have a big harvest festival. That's what they did in lieu of football."

"Where did you go after that?"

"I moved to Clarksburg, West Virginia," Frank continued, "where I became the weekend anchor and reporter. This was market number one hundred fifty, so I had made a nice jump up in the TV market rankings. I stayed there for about a year and a half, then moved to Lynchburg, Virginia, which was market number seventy-five. I was the weekend anchor."

"You were moving up at a pretty good pace."

"Yes, I was. News was my passion so I didn't mind the ten- to twelve-hour days. It was exciting, fulfilling, and rewarding. I was well on my way to achieving my ultimate career goal of working in one of the top twenty TV markets.

"Though I only stayed in Lynchburg for nine months, it was to be a turning point in my career. This was the late eighties, and Jerry Falwell with his Moral Majority were making headlines regularly. I did a lot of news stories about Falwell, and in the course of covering him I had lots of interesting conversations. He was Southern Baptist and I was (and still am) Catholic. I think he was kind of fascinated with me because you don't find many Catholics in the South. We had a great working relationship.

"One day, Falwell called me from his plane to tell me about fellow evangelist Jim Bakker, whose tawdry personal life was about to hit the fan. 'Can I run with this story?' I asked Falwell. 'Sure,' he replied. So I pulled together my story and put it on the evening news. It was huge."

"What an adventure!" I exclaimed.

"It was very exciting. But the story gets even better. I didn't know it, but the news director from Norfolk, Virginia, happened to be in town and he saw me do the Bakker story that night. A couple of weeks later he called to tell me that he liked what he saw and did I want to come work for him in Norfolk."

"Did you go?"

"You bet I did. Norfolk was market number forty-one. It was a great career move and I stayed there for four and a half years.

"Then I moved to Baltimore, Maryland, as a reporter and the bureau chief in Annapolis, the state capitol. Baltimore was a huge city compared to Toledo, where I grew up. And I had another great adventure there: Pope John Paul was supposed to visit Baltimore, but just before his trip, he fell and broke a hip, so his trip was canceled. I was on good terms with the archbishop for our area, since I covered church stories every so often. He told me he was going to Rome to invite the pope to reschedule his visit for the following year, after recovering from the hip fracture. He was going to take gifts for John Paul and give them to him, along with the invitation. 'Can I go with you?' I asked the archbishop. 'I'd love to do a story for our local news.'"

"You don't have a problem with shyness, do you?" I teased Frank.

"In my business, you can't afford to be shy and retiring," he responded. "When you see a story, you have to reach for it. And I knew there was a potential story here, so I pursued it. I had to ask again and again. The archbishop wasn't sure it was such a good idea, so he kept putting me off. Then finally, the weekend before Thanksgiving, he called me from Rome. 'If you can be here by Wednesday, I'll let you come with me when I go see Pope John Paul.'

"I asked my news director, who said, 'Go for it.' So I took a photographer with me and we flew to Rome. On Wednesday, we accompanied the archbishop to see the pope and present the gifts along with an invitation to come to Annapolis. It was just the three of us. 'Who are you?' the pope asked when he saw me. I introduced myself and my photographer and told him that we were doing a story about the invitation and proposed visit to our city. John Paul smiled and said, 'If it's not on TV, it doesn't really happen.' Then he added, 'I'll see you next year.' "

"Wow, that's an amazing story. And for you, being Catholic, it must have been especially wonderful."

"Yes, it was," Frank replied. "It was life-changing."

"How so?"

Frank thought for a minute before replying. "Meeting the pope made me think about bigger things. Up until now, it was all about my career—about making it to a top-twenty market. But now I began to think about other aspects of life.

"My wife and I had had our first child, and I could feel my priorities begin to shift. My mother's health was starting to fail—I'm an only child and I wanted to be closer to her. Family concerns were tugging at me.

"At the same time, the TV news business was changing. In the old days it was about great storytelling. Now it was changing to: 'Get it on the air, get it done, then move on.' I was working ten hours a day, every day of the week, but I could feel at times the passion wasn't there anymore. The business was changing, my family was changing, and I was changing."

"So what did you do?"

"I moved to Cincinnati to be closer to my mom in Toledo, just a few hours away. There were race riots in Cincinnati in the spring of 2001. There had been a police shooting and parts of the city erupted in violence. I was out there on the street, covering the story, when I heard a woman yelling, 'Mr. Graff! Mr. Graff!' It was a woman who had moved from Baltimore to Cincinnati to get away from crime and violence, and she recognized me from seeing me on TV. Suddenly we got shot at, and both of us hit the ground as the bullets whizzed over us. *This is a great story*, I thought to myself. *Here is a woman who moved from Baltimore to Cincinnati to escape violence, and now she's in the middle of a race riot.* I led the news with her story that night.

"It was scary and terrific at the same time. I won a local Emmy for that story—then won the first national Emmy ever awarded to a local reporter. My photographer and I went to New York the next year to attend the Emmy Awards. Barbara Walters presented the plaque. The ceremony also happened to fall on the first anniversary of 9/11, so we stayed in New York and covered stories of Cincinnati firefighters who had gone to New York to help after the attacks."

"You've had some incredible experiences."

"Yes. I spent the next four years in Cincinnati. But during that time, my wife and I traveled to North Carolina for a wedding. We were both impressed by the people, the community, and the countryside. What a great place to raise kids, we said to each other. So we moved here in 2004 after I landed a job with an NBC-owned station in Raleigh. A network station! This was the top of the heap. I'd achieved my goal.

"But somehow, it wasn't the thrill I thought it would be. Somewhere along the way, I'd lost my passion for TV news. My passion was now my family.

"A year after arriving, the station was sold, so it was no longer an NBC station. It was clear the station was changing as the business was changing, and a couple of years later the new owners took away my photographer. I was now what's called a one-man band—writing the story, doing the interview, shooting the story, editing it, and running it. This was just like the early days when I had worked in small local stations, having to do it all myself. I knew then that this was a sign it was time for me to leave—it was time to do something else."

"Like what?"

"I didn't know," Frank replied. "On Ash Wednesday of this year I was interviewing the local Catholic bishop for an Easter story. 'Are you OK?' he asked me. 'You don't seem like yourself.' I told him what was going on. I explained how I was sending out dozens of résumés and trying my best to figure out what to do next. I'll never forget his words—he said simply, 'Sometimes you need to stop looking and just listen.'

"So I took his advice and relaxed. I trusted that the answer would come in the right way, in the right time. Then one day, my intuition prompted me to pick up the phone and call 919 Marketing, a marketing/public relations firm in Holly Springs, a community near Raleigh. I had done some stories on a few of their clients in the past and I liked the way they worked. The owner, David Chapman, was very understanding of what I was going through, and even though I hadn't worked in public relations, I knew media. He gave me a chance. So three months ago I quit my TV job and came to work for 919 Marketing."

"So you've gone from being in front of the camera to pitching other people to be on camera."

"Yes, and it's been a huge change. I've had to learn all kinds of skills I never had to learn before, especially computer skills. Excel, Word, PowerPoint—these are all things I didn't have to know before. And I'm forty-eight years old."

"What else is different?"

"Time. Time is different in this job. In TV news I thought of myself as having a 'story canvas' to paint, with only a minute and a half to do it. Everything about the news business is fast, and it provides instant gratification. In this marketing job, my biggest challenge has been to slow down. The timeline for projects is much longer and I have plenty of time to do them. In marketing, you only get one chance to make a good impression, so you take your time and prepare well. So slowing down is still an adjustment I'm making.

"But there have been some really positive things about this career change, too. After twenty-five years in the news business, I actually had Thanksgiving off for the first time. Christmas, too. It was wonderful. The children loved it. And at the same time, I have to admit that it felt odd. *What do I do now?* I kept wondering."

"Do you think you'll stay in marketing?"

"I don't know yet," Frank replied. "It's too soon to tell. I'm enjoying learning new skills. I'm very much in the process of reinventing myself, of redefining who I am. As for the future—who knows?"

"Your story is different from most other career change stories," I observed. "Other people tell me that they worked for years in jobs they didn't like, all the while squelching their real passion. Then, finally, they decide to follow their passion and do what they really love.

"Your story is just the opposite. You pursued your passion from the get-go and after twenty-five years, the passion disappeared. That's really interesting. What advice would you give others who might find themselves in a similar situation?"

Frank thought for a minute before he answered. "Well, I remember something that a friend of mine told me after our daughter was born. 'You can still do everything you used to do before you had children, everything just takes longer.' I think of those words often as I learn these new skills.

"And I'd tell people to follow their hearts—follow their passion. And pay attention if the passion ever disappears, or changes. It's not that every day at work, or in life, is going to be an amazing, incredible day. That's not real life, that's not realistic. Even the saints had bad days. But you still need to have that passion to stay energized and be true to yourself and believe in what you're doing. In my case, my passion shifted from my career to my family, so I'm following that.

"I also like the words of advice that the bishop gave me: 'Stop looking and just be quiet and listen.' I do think God will provide that guidance so you'll intuitively know the right thing to do when it's time to do it."

Frank Graff is an account executive at 919 Marketing.
To contact him, go to www.919marketing.com.

One doesn't discover new lands without consenting to lose sight of the shore for a very long time.

—André Gide, French author and Nobel laureate

EASY RIDING THROUGH CAREER CHANGES

"The odyssey of Dennis Hopper has been one of Hollywood's longest, strangest trips," claims the celebrity website www.dennis-hopper.com. "A one-time teen performer, he went through a series of career metamorphoses—studio pariah, rebel filmmaker, drug casualty, and comeback kid—before finally settling comfortably into the role of character actor par excellence, with a rogue's gallery of killers and freaks unmatched in psychotic intensity and demented glee."

Now in his 70s, Hopper seems to be still crazy after all these years.

But despite his success as an actor and director, Hopper says that he sees himself primarily as an artist. He is an avid collector, as well as a painter and photographer. Largely unknown in the US art world, he's made a name for himself overseas.

In 2008, Hopper became the first living American artist to exhibit at the fabled Hermitage gallery in St. Petersburg, Russia. He told starpulse.com, "At the Hermitage, they had five rooms there with my work and it was incredible. I'm the most famous American artist in Russia, and nobody knows my artwork in the United States. The Cinémathèque in Paris is getting ready to do this show. They're taking half of my art collection and half of my own stuff and filling a whole room with a virtual reality exhibit....It's just amazing. I can't wait to see it all."

Hopper began painting in the 1950s, influenced by fellow actor Vincent Price, who also had a passion for art. His early works were Abstract Impressionist, and his artist friends included Jasper Johns, David Hockney, and Roy Lichtenstein. He was also influenced by James Dean, who "spearheaded the idea that acting was only one aspect of art, and to do painting and photography is also important." (www.Washingtonpost.com, April 1, 2006, article by William Booth)

A disastrous fire in 1961 destroyed his Los Angeles home and all of his paintings, about 300. That might have been the end of his art. But his wife gave him a camera after the fire—and, like a phoenix rising from the ashes, Hopper embraced a new art form, black-and-white photography.

Today, he continues to move seamlessly from one art form to another. He acts; he paints; he directs; he photographs; he does commercials; he hobnobs with world-famous artists. Hopper is still an easy rider, cruising through his career and life—the quintessential free spirit.

TRADEOFFS

Bob Levine had it all—a big, beautiful house that was paid off, a thriving law partnership, a beautiful, intelligent wife as the administrator of his law practice, and two grown kids whose educations (including grad school) he had been able to pay for. Bob and wife Sue had no debt, no financial worries, and by all appearances, not a care in the world.

So what would make them decide to sell the law practice, give up their careers, sell their gorgeous home, leave their friends, and move to another city where they had no jobs and no house? They were both over 50—not exactly spring chickens.

Other people might have thought that Bob and Sue were crazy, but they knew that their life in Northridge, California, wasn't as picture-perfect as it looked. After 30 years of self-employment, the stress of being a high-powered trial attorney was beginning to take its toll on Bob's health. "I'm a guy who takes things seriously," Bob said. "I'm not someone who can just lighten up, even when I know I should. I had sixteen lawyers working for me, and our firm had multimillion dollars in billable hours each year. That's a lot of responsibility.

"But I knew that my dad had three major heart attacks before age fifty, and I didn't want to suffer the same fate. My work was stressful; our Los Angeles suburban community became more and more congested; the local traffic was a nightmare. Was I going to ruin my own health for the sake of a fat paycheck? Something had to change—I could just feel it.

"Our son had moved to Santa Barbara after graduate school, so Sue and I spent plenty of time visiting—and we loved it. We enjoyed the ocean, the mountains, the charming small city, and the more relaxed pace of life. So we put a plan in place. This wasn't something sudden or impulsive—that's not our style. Changing our lifestyle was a process. We took baby steps.

"We bought a condo in Santa Barbara, and I commuted three days a week back to Woodland Hills for my law practice. Housing prices in Northridge were depressed due to the big earthquake in 1994—we lived at the quake's epicenter, 91325—so we weren't in any big hurry to sell our home. By 2003, the market had rebounded, so we listed the house with a Realtor. I sold my law practice to my partners and that was the end of that.

"Sue and I were in good shape financially, but we weren't rich by any means. If I could have held on to my business for another five years, I would probably never have had to work again. But I just didn't want to take that chance with my health. I needed to make the move sooner rather than later.

"We put a pencil to the numbers—we figured I could take three years off before I would need to start making some money again. It was very relaxing. I took some classes, joined a few groups, and became handy fixing things around the house. But I found that after a year and a half, I was getting bored. I needed to look for something to do.

"Sue had already figured out what she wanted to do next. She was a retired librarian who often found herself doing research for family and friends—research came naturally to her, and she took to the Internet like a fish to water. But for many people, especially older people, venturing out onto the Web was too intimidating, too daunting. So Sue decided to start a new business—a one-stop website that would link fifty-somethings easily and precisely with the information they needed. She called it 50somethinginfo.com and launched it late last year. She loves the process of building a business from scratch—dealing with challenges that she never encountered as a librarian working for someone else.

"I'd been self-employed for thirty years, and I'd had enough of those challenges. But I hadn't looked for a job since 1974, so I was at a bit of a loss as to how to go about it. What am I looking for in a job? I asked myself. I like to deal with people, but I don't want to work in an office. I've long been interested in cars, so a job having to do with cars would be fun, I thought. I saw an ad in the local newspaper for a salesman wanted—it was for a car dealership. I went for an interview and was hired on the spot.

"It was a huge transition—going from being a business owner to low man on the totem pole. But I discovered that my skills as a trial lawyer were invaluable in my new role. In a trial, I always have to think two steps ahead: One, I have to anticipate what's going to be said, and two, I have to think about building a case for an appeal after this trial is over. In the car business, I only have to think *one* step ahead.

"I had to learn about the cars I was selling, as well as the competition, and that was new. But other things were not new: I knew how to anticipate needs; I knew how to talk to people; and I knew the importance of listening. I may have started off at the bottom of the heap in that dealership, but it didn't take long before my skills took me to the top. Today, I'm their top-selling salesman."

When I asked Bob what advice he and Sue have for people who want to make a big change in their lives, he said, "For others, the change might be made easier because they got laid off or fired—they have no choice but to change. For me, the fear factor was enormous—I gave up something really successful and launched out into the unknown. Coming to grips with fear is what I'd advise people to do. It helps to remind yourself that you're not the first one to make a big change, and that others have done it and been successful."

Bob thought about his answer for a moment, then added, "One thing that helped Sue and me was the fact that we were accustomed to my *not* having regular paychecks. So the irregular income of a car salesman has not been a problem for us."

For more information about Sue Levine's new
business serving boomers and seniors, visit her website:
www.50somethinginfo.com.

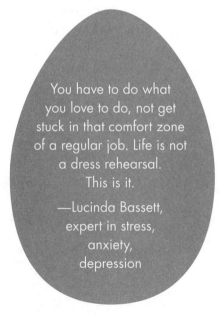

You have to do what
you love to do, not get
stuck in that comfort zone
of a regular job. Life is not
a dress rehearsal.
This is it.

—Lucinda Bassett,
expert in stress,
anxiety,
depression

NEVER-TOO-LATE TIPS FOR
STARTING A NEW CAREER

1.
If you knew you had only one year to live, is this the career you'd want to be in? Listen to your heart as well as your head. Start thinking about and moving toward the job or career that would really fulfill you.

2.
Conduct informational interviews with people who are doing the kind of work you think you'd like to do. Learn from their experiences.

3.
Find a way to try out the prospective new career before you actually commit to it. Perhaps you can do it part-time while you still keep your present job. Consider an internship or apprenticeship to see if the work is as satisfying as you think it would be.

4.
Some career changes require training and education, and other career changes don't. Do some research and find out what academic credentials, if any, are required for the work you want to do.

5.
The best jobs are those that are a little too big for you. They force you to stretch and grow. Welcome the challenge of new jobs or careers that will test you and push you in positive ways.

CHAPTER 3

IT'S NEVER TOO LATE TO GO BACK TO SCHOOL

The wisest mind has something yet to learn.

—*George Santayana,*
philosopher, poet, cultural critic

When I was a little girl, my favorite game was "school." Fifty years later, it still is.

I love ideas and theories, research studies and experiments, interesting lectures and stimulating discussions. I feel at home in classrooms, libraries, labs, and study halls. I feel totally jazzed when I'm learning something new. There are few things that thrill me more than the process of discovery. I dig chalkboards and whiteboards, three-ring binders and peachy folders, yellow legal pads and ballpoint pens, laptops and overhead projectors. I love everything about school.

If I can't be the student, then I'll be the teacher. If I can't make my living reading books, then I'll write them. If attending seminars won't pay the bills, then I'll lead the seminars. I don't care—as long as I get to play school.

Now, I realize that not everyone feels as I do about education. Some prefer learning on the job or simply learning from Life. I don't think it really matters where you learn, as long as you do learn.

LIFELONG LEARNING

"I always wanted to study anthropology," Jennie Richards told me, "but my father insisted I do something in the field of business instead, so I got my degree in advertising. You see, my two older brothers both had financial difficulties, and so Dad was concerned about my ability to be self-supporting. My older brother and sister at various times needed financial support from my father, so my father wanted me to be totally financially independent—thus the business-oriented degree.

"I lived in Avignon, France, for a year on an academic exchange program, and that intensified my hunger to learn more about cultures and international relations, thinking perhaps I could work in international business."

"So, what did you do when you finished your degree?" I asked her.

"When I graduated from the University of Washington, I got a job as a copywriter and account executive for an advertising agency, but after working several years in advertising I knew it wasn't what I really wanted to do," Jennie replied. "So I took a year off to travel South and Central America, and when I returned to Seattle I decided to return to school. I wanted to improve my writing and I also longed to read the world's great books, so I decided to study literature and earn a second degree."

"What was it like, going back to school after being out in the working world?"

"I was twenty-six when I returned to school, a few years older than my classmates," Jennie said, "and I noticed that I was more focused, more serious about my coursework than the younger students."

"Did getting another degree change your career?"

"Yes and no. My confidence in my writing improved significantly, but it was more about wanting to do something for my own personal growth and edification. I didn't want to go through life not having read the most famous literature and poetry ever written. But in truth, this course of study and degree still didn't reflect my vocational yearning to work internationally and somehow make a difference in the world. However, looking back, it has helped me immensely throughout my career because strong writing has been very important."

"You love to travel, don't you?"

"Yes, I do," Jennie said. "Fourteen years later, at age forty, I took another year off and this time headed east—to central and southern Asia. I spent a couple of months in Australia, then traveled through the islands of Indonesia, Malaysia, and Thailand, and then my father suddenly died. So I flew home and spent several months taking care of my mother before leaving again to finish my travels, reconfiguring a new itinerary due to weather. I started in Greece this time for a month, then a month in Turkey, and on to Egypt, India, Nepal, Cambodia, Vietnam, and Thailand for seven months. Fortunately my sister was able to care for my mother while I was gone, which allowed me to finish the trip. But when I returned I moved back to Seattle from Boston to care for my Mom until the end of her life.

"When I came back from my year abroad, I started working again, this time doing brand and product management and launching two Internet websites. I worked full-time and took care of Mom until she died two years later."

"Did that change anything for you?"

"That's when I got hired by LVMH/Sephora (Louis Vuitton Moët Hennessy) and relocated to San Francisco to became the executive producer and launch the website Sephora.com. It was a great and challenging job and I stayed for eight years, but I still longed to do something that was more meaningful, purposeful, and would make a positive difference in the world. It became very clear to me that working in 'business-as-usual' corporations just wasn't very fulfilling or satisfying. I also became increasingly concerned with global warming, species decline, and the rapid deterioration of the world's forests and environment. This was pulling at me, and I found I was drawn to attend lectures and programs that addressed these topics—and when I found an MBA in Sustainable Enterprise at Dominican University of California, it was like a light went off!

"And now here I am—fifty-two years old—and back in school for the third time. I have to tell you, this is the hardest program I've ever been in. I've always been a straight-A student, but this MBA is more demanding, more consuming, than any other academic work I've done. But you know what? I'm doing what I've always wanted to do—finally. So even though I'm working harder than I've ever worked, I'm happier than I've ever been."

"What advice would you give people who might be thinking about going back to school?"

"I'd tell them it's never too late. It takes strong self-esteem and confidence in yourself to know that you can go back to school—even though you've been out of the academic world for many, many years and everyone is much younger—and to stay with it—and stay focused on it and not give anyone the power to derail your intention and goal.

"I didn't want to live with regrets," Jennie continued. "My subconscious had never let go of the idea of making a difference in the world, so I knew it was right to leave my job. For the past twenty years I have wanted to work at something I love, and I finally trusted that I could do it.

"I'd say that the timing has to be right to go back to school. I've grown a lot by taking this program when I was ready. I wasn't as ready when I was younger, and I would have been less like a sponge to all the learning that was possible.

"It's never too late to do something that your heart really desires. I didn't get married until I was forty-five. Now I'm back in school at age fifty-two. My life is proof that you don't have to follow a set template or do what everyone else does, just because they do it. It's so important to follow your own internal guide and intuition about what is right for you—and then just do it! It doesn't matter your age, just as long as you're being true to your own internal compass. I think that the right time to do what you love is when you're ready."

A college education is not a quantitative body of knowledge salted away in a card file. It is a taste for knowledge, a taste for philosophy, if you will—a capacity to explore, to question, to perceive relationships, between fields of knowledge and experience.

—A. Whitney Griswold,
president of Yale University

The purpose of the university is to make students safe for ideas—
not ideas safe for students.

—Clark Kerr, former president of the
University of California

IT'S NEVER TOO LATE TO
LEARN...

LISTEN with an open mind.
EXPERIMENT with new ideas.
ASK good questions.
READ, read, read.
NEVER STOP being curious.

A happy life is one spent
in learning, earning, and
yearning.

—Lillian Gish, actress

Learning is a treasure that will follow its owner everywhere.

—Chinese proverb

HEEDING THE CALL OF
THE WILD BLUE YONDER

A woman's place is—in the cockpit? I was curious to learn more about a woman who took up flying in midlife. It wasn't exactly everyone's notion of "going back to school." But then, there are many kinds of schools—not just academic ones.

"What was your career goal when you were a girl?" I asked Elgene Doinidis at the beginning of our conversation. "Have you always wanted to be a pilot?"

"No," she replied. "I actually wanted to be an airline stewardess—now they are referred to as flight attendants. I did some research about the requirements when I was in high school and was disappointed to learn that stewardesses had to be five feet two inches tall and weigh at least a hundred ten pounds. Well, I was only five feet tall, and very tiny, so that was the end of that. I wasn't ever going to be a stewardess."

"But now you're a pilot," I said. "How did that happen?"

"In 1996, my husband and I attended a fund-raising event at School-craft College in Livonia, Michigan. The event consisted of a silent auction, and my husband and I often enjoy the bidding process. This time, one of the items we bid on was a flight in a small airplane. And guess what? We won it.

"The plane was owned by a pilot in Northville, Michigan. A few weeks after the silent auction, we met him at the airport in Monroe, Michigan, where he kept his plane. The three of us flew to Put-In-Bay, located in the middle of Lake Erie. We landed, got out of the plane, walked around the island a bit, then got back into the plane for our return flight.

"I remember it was a gorgeous day—crystal-clear skies, beautiful weather, and the sights were incredible. We flew at about four or five thousand feet. The view was like nothing I'd ever seen before. At one point, we were flying just five hundred feet above the water and it was simply breathtaking.

"On our way back, the pilot asked me if I wanted to fly the plane, and I said no. I had no idea how to fly a plane and the thought of it scared me. But he reassured me, 'Just take the controls in front of you and steer.' I was in front next to him while my husband was in the back seat. 'That's all you have to do. It's easy.'

"So I did. And he was right—it was easy, exciting, and fun."

"Sounds like a wonderful adventure."

"It was," Elgene replied, nodding. "I had so much fun that after we landed and were walking back to our car, I turned to my husband and said, 'You know what? I'd like to learn how to fly!' I'll never forget his response: 'Aren't you too old?'

"That was all it took, for him to tell me I was too old to learn to fly. I was fifty-four years old and nobody was going to tell me I was too old for anything!"

Elgene and I both laughed. "Ain't it the truth," I said. "The surest way to get somebody to do something is to tell them they can't."

"I started doing research into flight schools in the area," she continued. "I found one in Plymouth, Michigan, at Mettetal Airport. I began to learn to fly there in a Cessna 152 but then decided I would like to learn at a larger airport with a control tower, so I would become comfortable with communications between me and the controller. I also thought it would be helpful for me to learn flying with a female instructor.

"I did more research and found an airport in Ann Arbor, as well as a terrific woman instructor. Her name was Jana and we were perfectly suited. I felt very comfortable relating woman to woman as I learned about aviation, a world totally foreign and new to me. Jana and I met a couple of times a week to study 'ground school' and to learn flying skills. She was a lot younger than I was—probably in her thirties—but that didn't matter. We did lots of girl things, talking, laughing and having fun going up in the plane to just 'poke some holes in the sky.' It was a great relationship and a beautiful experience."

"When did you get to solo?" I asked.

"To complete your pilot license, you have to learn a number of things: how the plane works, the flying environment, and 'how to fly' from your instructor. Students solo when the instructor feels you're ready. I had about thirty hours flying with Jana and I had the feeling that the solo was coming up soon, but, as with most students, I never knew exactly when.

"One day, she and I were up in the plane—I was piloting and she was in the copilot seat. We landed and she said, 'Pull the plane over to the Aviation Center. I need to go to the bathroom, so let me just run in there for a minute and I'll be right out.'

"I waited in the plane while she went inside the Aviation Center. A few minutes later she came out of the building carrying a little teddy bear that was wearing an aviator's cap and bomber jacket. She opened the door of the plane, put the teddy bear on the seat where she'd been sitting, and said, 'Now you're going to go up alone. I want you to think of this teddy bear as Jana and remember all the things I taught you and that I'm there with you.' "

"Aw, that's so sweet," I said. "Only a woman would think of doing something as thoughtful as that."

"Yes, it made me feel really good," Elgene replied. "And it was still scary. I taxied to the runway, held short as instructed by the controller. I requested to 'stay in the pattern'—basically a long rectangle in the sky a thousand feet above the ground. Then I looked at that teddy bear and thought, *I must be crazy!* I took off, did three perfect full-stop landings. Jana signed off on my first solo flight. I was now authorized to fly solo as a student pilot.

"That is a great story. Just terrific!"

"It was a big day for me, for sure," Elgene said. "But my training wasn't over. After your first solo, there is more instruction. You have to finish ground school and take a written Federal Aviation Administration exam. You are also required do some cross-country solos, short and long. I flew to Marshall, Michigan, for my first cross-country by just following the road below, I-94.

"For my long cross-country solo, I decided to fly to Alpena, Michigan, where my parents lived. This was June of 1998 and I was now fifty-six. I wanted to visit them on Father's Day and show my mom and dad that I could really fly. It was a big deal—a hundred seventy-eight nautical miles from Ann Arbor. I followed the road below, which led me to Flint, then on to Bay City, where I landed. I had planned to stop there, just in case the flight was proving to be too long and I might need to turn back. I'll never forget, I got out of the plane and told the guy at the airport, 'I'd like some fuel.' 'Who's the pilot?' he asked. 'I am!' I said proudly. He looked surprised to see this tiny little woman, barely five feet tall, piloting this plane.

"After gassing up, I took off again and flew the rest of the way to Alpena, where my mom and dad met me at the airport. They walked out onto the tarmac where I had parked the plane, and Dad asked me to turn the engine on again. When I did, he looked at me and said, 'That thing sounds like a lawn mower!' We all laughed.

"Mom told me something I'd never known before: when she graduated from country normal school many years earlier, Amelia Earhart had been the commencement speaker! In her speech, Earhart told the graduating students that if they ever had a chance to fly in a small plane to see a sunrise or sunset, they should jump at the opportunity. There's nothing in the world quite like it, Earhart said.

"Isn't that something? I asked Mom why she had never told me that before, and she said, 'There was never any reason to.' It just seemed to me that there was some kind of cosmic connection going on here—it was a special day in more ways than one."

"Wow, that *is* amazing."

"My life has been a whole series of amazing things since my husband and I took that first flight we'd won in the silent auction," Elgene continued. "Jana left Michigan and went to Alaska to become a bush pilot, so I now found yet another terrific woman instructor, Shelly. One day she was telling me about a female pilot she'd just met who was looking for a partner to share half the cost of her plane. This was 1998 or '99, and the lady was a professor at the University of Michigan. I thought about it for a while and talked to my husband about it. He was very encouraging. Then, a few days later, when we were having dinner at home, there next to my salad plate was a stack of hundred-dollar bills—a hundred forty of them—totaling fourteen thousand dollars, the cost of my half of the Piper Cherokee."

"This story just gets better and better," I interjected. "Your husband must be quite a guy."

"He is," Elgene said with a smile. "Other than that first comment when he questioned whether I was too old to fly, he's been a hundred percent supportive.

"So the whole flying thing has been more than I ever could have dreamed. Someone once described Amelia Earhart as 'not terribly gifted—she just perseveres.' I think that describes me, too. I went on to get certified to fly in instrument conditions—that is, in the clouds. This rating is referred to as an instrument rating. Now I felt I was truly a pilot.

"In 2001, I bought my own airplane, a Mooney, which was quite a bit more expensive than the first plane I had been sharing. My parents had put money aside for years for my brother and me. 'It's for when you get older and want a retirement home,' my dad told me. I said, 'I don't want a retirement home, Dad. I want a plane of my own!' So I used my inheritance to purchase a plane.

"In my parents' honor, I designated a new tail number for my plane, N102PL. N means the plane is registered in the United States. 10-2 is the date of my birth; P is for my mother, Phyllis; and L for my dad, Louis. Her name is *Whisper*, and this plane has become part of our family."

"They were clearly very proud of you."

"Yes, and I did everything I could to justify their pride in me and flying," Elgene replied. "At Schoolcraft College, where I am employed as a director, we recently designed an Aviation Management Program. The Aviation Management online program provides a broad perspective of aviation businesses, operations, airports, regulations, and a basic aircraft/flight overview with a blend of academic classes in aviation, business, and management. We have fifty-four students enrolled in the program, many of them pilots. Prior to learning to fly, I earned my master's degree in business in 1989. Here I am now, incorporating my avocation into my vocation. I took this dream of flying and made it part of my professional career."

"What advice would you give others who want to learn a new skill?"

"If you have a dream, you owe it to yourself to follow it," Elgene said. "Do your research; be selective; be persistent. Find the right school for you; then find the right instructors. And once you've begun learning your new skill and pursuing your new interest, be open to where it can take you. You might be very pleasantly surprised."

For more information about the aviation management program that Elgene Doinidis designed, visit the website: www.schoolcraft.edu/programs/avm.

The purpose of learning is growth, and our minds, unlike our bodies, can continue growing as long as we live.

—Mortimer Adler, philosopher, educational theorist

FAT ALBERT GOES TO COLLEGE

One might think that with a successful career in show business, a comedian wouldn't bother with formal education. And if that comedian achieved the level of fame and fortune that Bill Cosby did, why on earth would he want to pursue advanced degrees?

Cosby, a self-described class clown, dropped out of high school in 1956, after failing the tenth grade, and joined the US Navy. While serving as a hospital corpsman, he worked in physical therapy with seriously injured Korean War casualties. This experience helped him discover the need for an education, so he finished his high school equivalency diploma via correspondence courses. After his discharge from the Navy in 1961 he returned to his hometown of Philadelphia and enrolled in Temple University, winning an athletic scholarship. But as he discovered his gift for making people laugh, he dropped out in his sophomore year to pursue a career in comedy.

His 1963 appearance on *The Tonight Show* with Johnny Carson garnered enormous public attention. At a time of racial turmoil in the country, Cosby portrayed himself as Everyman, focusing on finding humor in everyday situations common to all people. "A white person listens to my act and laughs as he thinks, *Yeah, that's the way I see it too.* Okay. He's white. I'm Negro. And we both see things the same way. That must mean we are alike. Right? So I figure I'm doing as much good for race relations as the next guy." (*Cosby: The Life of a Legend*, by Ronald Smith.)

Two years later, he was cast in a leading role with Robert Culp in *I Spy*, for which he won three Emmy Awards. His TV career established, he continued with a series of successful shows: *Bill Cosby Specials* (1968–71), *The Bill Cosby Show* (1969–71), *The New Bill Cosby Show* (1972–73), the long-running *Fat Albert and the Cosby Kids* (1972–84), and the acclaimed *The Cosby Show* (1984–92).

Yet with the enormous demands of a Hollywood career, he still made time to continue his education. He finally finished his BA at Temple, and went on to earn a master's degree in Education from the University of Massachusetts at age 35, and a PhD at age 40. He has since been awarded honorary degrees from Harvard, Yale, Baylor, Carnegie Mellon, and Berklee College of Music, among other institutions.

To this day, Cosby is an outspoken advocate for education, self-respect, and self-improvement. His own life is a testament to his message—few people walk their talk the way Cosby does.

RECOVERING
FROM CHILDHOOD

I know very few people who received the kind of unconditional love and support that we all wanted and needed from our parents. Most of us spend many years recovering from thoughtless comments, well-intentioned but hurtful criticism, and harsh judgments. Most people carry around old wounds that haunt them, even decades later. These painful stories are all too common. Jill Goodfriend's is such a story.

"My parents divorced when I was just a toddler. My mother remarried, but my stepfather wasn't much help to me when I was young because Mom ruled the roost. She was a force to be reckoned with, and my stepdad placated her to keep the peace.

"It was assumed that Mom was the one who really 'knew me,' since I was her biological child. My stepdad was busy with his career, so he kind of stayed out of any active child rearing. Our family moved around a lot—he was in the diplomatic corps and we lived in many exotic places. We moved to Indonesia when I was nine, and at age fourteen I began two years in boarding school while my parents lived in India. It seems that I was always either ahead or behind the other kids in my class, because my birthday is in December, which puts me at the cutoff age for grade assignments. I felt like I never fit in. I finally graduated from high school in 1963."

"Did you go on to college?" I asked.

"Dad—I call him Dad because he's the one I grew up with—had a college degree but my mother didn't," Jill replied. "She'd only completed high school. I always wanted to be a doctor and I recall that while other kids played house or played school, I just wanted to play doctor.

"But in those days, there were only three career options open to women: airline stewardess, nurse, or teacher. And the only reason girls went to college was to get an 'MRS degree'—to find a husband and get married. My mother said, 'I want you to get married, but you also need to have a fallback option, in case something ever happens to your husband. You need to get trained in something so you'll have a way to support yourself if you have to.'

"In high school I did extremely well in chemistry and physics, and my teachers believed in my capabilities. I even remember one of my teachers coming to our house to lobby my mother to let me go to medical school. That kind of support and encouragement felt so good! But Mom wouldn't hear of it, so I enrolled in nursing school instead."

"Gender played a huge role in women's careers in those days, didn't it?" I asked.

"Yes, it did. I had two younger brothers, seven and twelve years younger, and they were parented and encouraged very differently. I think that my mother didn't want me to have options that she didn't have. Maybe there was a little competitiveness going on there, I don't know."

"Since you wanted a medical career, did you enjoy nursing school?"

"No, I hated it," Jill replied. "I got D's in all of my nursing classes. I found the nursing instructors harsh, cruel, duplicitous, and domineering—a lot like my mother. I earned B's and C's in the college classes I took, but I just barely passed the nursing classes. Finally, halfway through the program, I was told to leave. 'You're too immature,' they said."

"That *is* harsh."

"Yes, but I was glad to get out of there. I went to work in a dentist's office for a while, but ultimately went back to finish my nursing degree.

I was angry and depressed the whole time, but determined to finish what I had started. Part of it was I wanted to prove something to my mother, who had said to me, 'You're not college material.'"

"Ouch."

"Ouch, indeed," Jill rejoined. "When I graduated from nursing school, I married a man I had met in high school. He was in the diplomatic corps like my dad and we moved around a lot, to Vietnam, Cambridge, Ottawa, among other places. My husband wanted me to go back to school, but for his own reasons, not mine. 'I'm going to be an ambassador someday,' he said. He wanted his wife to have some kind of career status closer to his own—being a nurse didn't cut it. So I went back to school to please my husband. I decided to study psychology, since we had a young daughter and I was eager to learn all I could to be a better mother than the one I'd had. I enrolled in Carlton University while we were in Ottawa.

"My husband left me in 1974 and it took me a number of years to finish my degree. I was still doing it to prove something to him, just as I'd gone to nursing school to please my mother. I moved to Washington, DC, and finally got my degree there in 1979. It was a challenge because I had trouble completing things. I'd take a class but not write the paper, or I'd take a class and not do the final exam. I was still a nurse all this time, because it was the only work I could get."

"It sounds really hard."

Jill nodded. "It was. The turning point came in 1984 when my stepdad came through town and we had lunch together. He and my mother had long since split up, and he was now very supportive of me. I told him I wanted to go back to school and do something in the field of counseling. He told me to go ahead and he would pay for it. As I look back now, I see that he often believed in me even when I didn't. I enrolled in a clinical social work program at Catholic University in Washington and finished my MSW in 1986."

"What did you do after that?"

"I got my first job at Washington Hospital Center—the same hospital where I'd trained as a nurse all those years before! I was now especially employable, since I had both an RN and an MSW—they hired me to be a discharge planning specialist. My status now was completely different than it had been as a nurse. I wore street clothes with a white lab coat over them, while nurses in the old days wore those awful starched uniforms with little white caps on their heads.

"For the first time in my life, I felt that I'd arrived. No place in the hospital was off-limits to me; I had a great deal of status; and I'd learned a hell of a lot over the years that I brought to my new position. I was now a much bigger fish in that pond. I served as liaison between families, patients, and the doctors and nurses."

"Sounds like a very fulfilling job."

"Fulfilling, but also very intense and demanding," Jill replied. "After five years of it I burned out and developed chronic fatigue syndrome. I quit my job, spent the next two years focused solely on restoring my health. I got acupuncture and took herbal remedies. I pursued all sorts of medical paths in my pursuit of health. I did work part-time at a kids' summer camp, where I got to be outdoors and enjoy exercise, fresh air, and youthful activities.

"I am happy to report that I recovered fully and took a new job in mental health with Kaiser Permanente in Washington. I worked for them as a therapist. I had my own office and really liked it.

"But life often takes twists and turns because of unexpected events, and in 1990 I was RIFFed from my therapist job. I took it hard. But once I finished licking my wounds, I opened my own therapy practice, and much to my delight, some of my Kaiser patients wanted to continue to work with me, so they became my patients in private practice.

"Then another surprising twist—I got a part-time job doing consultations with Washington Hospital Center. Here I was once again, back at that same hospital! All told, I spent twenty-five years at the same hospital. Kind of ironic, don't you think?"

"Life *is* full of surprises and ironies," I agreed.

"But sometime later, while the hospital was undergoing recertification, it came to light that I was not current on my immunizations," Jill continued. "Regulations required that all hospital staff be up to date on their shots, and I wasn't. After much research and deliberation, I refused to take the shots—I was concerned about triggering another bout of chronic fatigue. As a result, I lost that job."

"Wow, your story has a definite roller-coaster quality to it."

"Well, here I was, fifty years old, with no job," she continued. "I figured it was the universe giving me a big push. I had always wanted to go to California, since we visited there once when I was ten. So I sold my house and moved west. Today I am sixty-four years old, and this is the first time in my life I'm living somewhere I want to live! Everywhere else I've lived in my life was dictated by my dad's or my husband's career.

"I had to get licensed in the state of California, and once I did that, I set up my private practice. I also became a nursing instructor at a couple of local nursing schools. And I started up some pet loss support groups, because I lost my old cat that moved with me from Washington. I do mental health volunteer work for the Red Cross whenever there's a crisis, like 9/11.

"And I have to tell you, the really funny thing is that today I am *valued* as a nurse, even though I haven't done any nursing in years!"

"With such a history of ups and downs, what would you advise others?"

"I'd suggest two things. First, go inside and listen to your true self, our higher self. We each know ourselves better than anyone else does—parents, family, or friends—if only we can believe in ourselves. The answers to our questions about life work are inside us—not outside.

"Second, gather as much information as you can about the school you want to attend, or the career you want to pursue. That way you can inform your intuition with logic."

The library is the temple of learning,
and learning has liberated more people
than all the wars in history.

—Carl T. Rowan, journalist and author

NEVER-TOO-LATE TIPS FOR GOING BACK TO SCHOOL

1.
Do your research and find the right school and instructors for you. Evaluate what each school offers and weigh it against the cost.

2.
Pace yourself. If you have to work full-time while you're going to school, be careful you don't burn out. It might be worthwhile to take fewer classes at once and take longer to finish your education.

3.
Remember that what you do outside the classroom is just as important as what you do in class. Consider extracurricular learning opportunities: internships, student government, campus leadership, student newspaper, special projects.

4.
You may not need to earn a degree or certificate to learn what you want. Sometimes just as class or two is plenty.

5.
Be clear about your motives for going to school. Are you doing it for yourself or to prove something to someone else?

CHAPTER 4

IT'S NEVER TOO LATE TO EXPRESS YOUR CREATIVITY

There is a vitality, a life force, an energy, a quickening that is translated through you into action. And because there is only one of you in all of time, this expression is unique. And if you block it, it will never exist through any other medium and be lost.

It is not your business to determine how good it is nor how valuable nor how it compares with other expressions.

It is your business to keep the channel open. Whether you choose to take an art class, keep a journal, record your dreams, dance your story, or live each day from your own creative source, above all else, keep the channel open!

—*Martha Graham, dancer, choreographer*

My mother was one of the most creative people I've known. When I was a little girl, Mom sometimes took me shopping. Every so often she would see something pretty that she particularly liked, but she wouldn't buy it. Instead, she'd eye it carefully, muttering softly to herself, "I can make that," and then she'd go home and fashion the almost identical item for herself. Our home was filled with lovely things that Mom had made—Christmas ornaments, refinished furniture, braided wool rugs, lamps made from antique objects, and more. She took great pride in both her ingenuity and her ability to save money and still get the things she wanted.

I'm convinced that everyone is creative. Some people are creative in the kitchen, whipping up interesting, tasty dishes by intuitively combining the right ingredients.

Other people are creative with mechanical things, with an uncanny ability to figure out the most complex engines or pieces of machinery. Some are handy with a sewing machine; others are skillful in building things. Creativity can express itself in the way a woman combines pieces of clothing or the way a man handles a wrench or saw.

Of course, creativity can also show up in the form of music, painting, pottery, sculpture, poetry, novels, or other writings. How one expresses one's creativity is almost limitless in terms of form. How do YOU express yours?

IN COMMAND OF HER ART

Adrienne van Dooren wasn't your typical college coed. While many young women were attracted to football players and frat boys, Adrienne was fascinated by cadets she saw rappelling out of a helicopter on campus. "That looked like great fun," she says today. "I was captivated by their sense of adventure. So I signed up for Army ROTC. That was 1979."

"That's a pretty unusual choice for a college girl," I said. "What did your parents think?"

"At that time it was a more unusual choice than it would be today," Adrienne replied. "I grew up believing there were only three options appropriate for women with a college degree: nursing, teaching, or homemaking. I planned to become a teacher so I majored in early childhood development. However, times were rapidly changing, and I realized there were a multitude of career options open to women, and the Army was actually more forward-thinking in that regard than society as a whole.

"When I told my mother I'd signed the contract for ROTC, she was very upset. She said, 'Only two kinds of women go join the Army.' In her view, females in the Army were either lesbians or those euphemistically referred to as 'loose women.' My father was happy with the choice because he knew how much I loved adventure."

"So upon graduation you had the option to go into the Army Reserves," I noted. "Why did you decide to go into the active duty Army full-time?"

"I joined the military for three reasons: One, the adventure: Rappelling out of helicopters, jumping from airplanes, and global travel really appealed to me. Two, to become more assertive: I was soft-spoken and shy, and I thought that military training would build my confidence and leadership abilities. Three, the challenge: Things had always come easy to me—good grades, et cetera—and I knew the military would push me to my limits and beyond, not just physically—push-ups, ten-mile marches, and running—but also as a leader."

"And did it?"

"Definitely. I got all that and more," Adrienne said. "I sometimes wonder what I would be like today had I not gone into the Army. The challenges, mentors, and travel have shaped me so completely. It started with ROTC; then, when I graduated in 1981, I was commissioned with a starting rank of second lieutenant and accepted to active duty. I shipped out to Arizona for the Military Intelligence Officer Basic Course."

"What's military intelligence?" I asked.

"Good question. When I chose military intelligence, I envisioned myself as Jane Bond, with a trench coat, a high-tech microphone in my shoe, and an exciting life of playing spy. But the Army assigned me to tactical intelligence. The Soviets were still perceived as the major threat in those days, so my job was to learn all I could about their military tactics, the kinds of combat units they had, their equipment, radars, et cetera. In short, tactical intelligence is supposed to help predict what the enemy might do next.

"After the Officer Basic Course, I shipped out to Rheinberg, Germany, which was a bit scary at first, since I didn't speak the language and would be living in a foreign country. But the Germans were really wonderful. In fact I've returned to Rheinberg every year since then to spend Christmas with a German family who sort of adopted me. After my two years in Rheinberg, I extended my time in Germany and was sent to Mannheim, where I served as the headquarters commander for a military police battalion.

"In 1986 I came back stateside to pursue a master's degree at the Defense College at DIA, in Washington, DC, which is affiliated with Georgetown University. I really liked Washington and would end up spending a lot of time there over the course of my military career.

"After finishing my master's, I was assigned to Fort Carson, Colorado, where I served as an intelligence staff officer and later became the division's protocol officer. I left Fort Carson a year early because I was selected for a Secretary of Defense Fellowship, and went to the Pentagon in 1990. At the Pentagon, I worked for Dick Cheney, who was the secretary of defense, and Colin Powell, chairman of the Joint Chiefs of Staff. It was clear that I was being fast-tracked for advancement—if I had chosen to stay on the fast track, I probably would have made it to general."

"Did your mom change her mind about your military career during any of this?"

"Oh, yes," Adrienne replied. "When I came back from Germany, my mother did a hundred-and-eighty-degree about-face. When I would go home to visit, she'd insist that I wear my uniform when we went to church on Sunday. She referred to me as 'my daughter, the general.' It was really funny."

"That must have felt good."

"Yes, it did. It means a lot when your parents are proud of you. But at the same time, Mom started talking about wanting grandkids. She blamed my career for my not having a husband or kids. There was some truth to that—it's hard to have a relationship when you're career military; there is just too much moving around and separation."

"Where did you go after the Pentagon?"

"I got an exciting and prestigious assignment as a White House aide and worked under Bush senior as well as Clinton. That was 1992–93.

"From there I went to Commander General Staff College at Fort Leavenworth, Kansas. I started dating a classmate, and we got engaged. My next tour of duty was to go back to Germany, but I decided I didn't want to go because it would have meant leaving my fiancé. I had also decided that I really wanted to teach, so I requested a teaching position at Leavenworth. I knew that in doing so, I wouldn't make lieutenant colonel, since teaching would derail my career track to senior ranks. But I made that choice. Unlike men, whose self-esteem depends so much on rank and status, my self-worth didn't. I loved teaching and helping people, and I decided that rank just wasn't that important to me.

"So I stayed at Leavenworth and started teaching at the staff college. And they actually had me design a course on creativity! I knew then that I was where I should be."

"That's pretty amazing."

"Yes, I thought so too," Adrienne agreed. "I was loving it. Unfortunately, the engagement didn't work out, so I wasn't so happy in my personal life, but my teaching work made me very happy.

"My last Army job was teaching ROTC in Fullerton, California, from 1998 to 2001. I loved California. I bought a couple of houses and renovated them—that was really creative. I learned to do tile, faux finishes, paint cabinetry, and much more, because I didn't have a lot of money so I needed to do it myself. That was my first taste of what I'm doing now."

"So, when did you leave the Army?"

"Well, it's interesting. For the first ten years of my military career, I loved it. But then I began to think about getting out, as my happiness diminished. Then one day I had a flat tire outside Las Vegas, Nevada, and a guy stopped to help me. We got to talking, and when I told him I was in the Army he said, 'Boy, I wish I had stayed in the Army. I only stayed seven years, but if I'd made it to twenty years, I could have been retired by now, and I wouldn't be changing tires for a living.' His comment really made me stop and think. I wanted the security of a steady income and a good retirement. So I stayed in for another ten years. But once I reached twenty years, I retired the first day I could so that I could have more freedom to be creative."

"What did you do then?"

"The VA had a retraining program to help people prepare for work in civilian jobs after retirement. But they didn't have a program for what

I wanted to do, which was faux finishing and decorative painting. So I did some research and came up with a proposal. I selected the top faux finishing schools across the country and then located a company that wrote a letter stating they would hire me if I completed ten one-week courses in various decorative painting specialties. I presented it to the VA and, much to my surprise, they okayed it. So I finished the training program, went to work for that company, and then after a few months went out on my own.

"Ironically, when I retired, I could barely draw a stick figure, but I found that art is more technique than talent. I believe anyone who has an eye for art can learn. I worked hard and got pretty good over time—decorative painting, oils, even portraits.

"Within five years I was at the top of my field. My work won awards and national recognition, and I was selected to teach at national painting conventions and schools across the US. I even wrote a book; it was titled *The House That Faux Built: Transform Your Home Using Paint, Plaster, and Creativity.* The book has sold very well, and all the book profits go to charity."

"That's a pretty dramatic career change—from Army officer to artist."

"It really was, but a lot of what I learned in the Army has stood me in good stead in the work I do today. I learned how to organize large projects, lead a team of artists, manage and motivate other people. Most of all, it gave me the knowledge that I could do anything I set my mind to. So in many ways, my military training was perfect.

"Also, military service is just that—service. It's about doing something to help others, protecting your country from danger. Service has always been important to me, so today I use my art to serve others. I started a group called Artists4Others and we do projects to raise money for animal rescue, we paint murals in hospice rooms, and we raised almost fifty thousand dollars for hurricane victims. Over one hundred artists participated, and that's where the book idea for *The House That Faux Built* came from."

"That's fabulous!" I said. "One last thing. What advice would you give others who are thinking about making a big change in their own lives?"

"Fear is the biggest block for most people," Adrienne replied. "I would suggest that they get to know other folks who are doing what they think they want to do. Talk to them and offer to work for free to get a feel for the job. Then decide if it's really the right move. If it is, just jump in. That's what I've done all my life. I jumped into the military; I jumped into Germany; I jumped into teaching; and I jumped into art. Luckily, I've always landed on my feet."

Adrienne van Dooren is an artist and author of
The House That Faux Built, whose profits go to supporting
victims of Hurricane Katrina.
Visit her website: www.fauxhouse.com.

Creative minds have always been known to survive any kind of bad training.

—*Anna Freud, psychotherapist,
daughter of Sigmund Freud*

Every artist makes herself born. You must bring the artist into the world yourself.

—*Willa Cather,
Pulitzer Prize-winning novelist*

IT'S NEVER TOO LATE TO
BE CREATIVE...

CULTIVATE an open mind, open eyes, open ears.

REACH for new experiences.

EXPLORE ideas.

ACT on impulse and intuition.

TAKE risks.

INVITE color and light into your life.

VEER away from conformity.

EXPRESS yourself.

Genius is essentially creative; it bears the stamp of the individual who possesses it.

—*Germaine de Staël,*
French author,
daughter of the Enlightenment

Life is raw material. We are artisans. We can sculpt our existence into something beautiful, or debase it into ugliness. It's in our hands.

—*Cathy Better,*
journalist, author, poet

A PASSION FOR CULINARY ARTS

Maria Liberati loves all things Italian. She grew up in a big Italian family in Philadelphia and attended college at Temple University. She had always been fascinated by her family's cultural heritage, intrigued by language, history, art, and food, and longed to learn more. Maria finally made her first trip to Italy when she was in her early 20s, and found it to be all she had dreamed of—and more.

Over the years, she spent more and more time in Italy, traveling there as often as she could. At first it was modeling gigs taking her to Rome; later it was travel to study and learn more about Italian culture and cuisine.

"I've been an entrepreneur all my life," Maria told me. "First while maintaining a successful modeling career, I started what became a successful special events/public relations company. Then I got into real estate investing."

"Did you major in business in college?" I asked her.

"No," she replied. "I majored in foreign language education, which prepared me to become a teacher of English as a second language. But in the back of my mind I knew I would never become a teacher, even though several family members were teachers.

"I spent about twenty years modeling, starting when I was twelve or thirteen, and it developed into a successful career. When I sold the special events company, the next logical thing seemed to be real estate investing, because it was the family business. But none of those things were my passion—not modeling, teaching languages, public relations, or real estate investing.

"My real passion is culinary arts. Italian food, in particular, is as much an artistic expression—as central to Italian culture—as the great sculpture, paintings, poetry, music, and other art forms. I think of myself as an artist. I write cookbooks that are also considered recipe novels because they include both recipes and memories—woven together in a lovely tapestry of flavor, family, and feelings."

"What advice would you give others?" I asked.

"It's not an easy thing to follow your passion later in life," Maria replied. "There are more naysayers—people who love you and are afraid for you. They seem to think that any creative vocation is ridiculous. It's not practical.

"It's important not to let other people discourage you from pursuing your lifelong passions. They may think they have your best interest at heart, but often they're afraid to pursue their own creativity. So they try to discourage you from doing it.

"You have to follow your own interests—do what makes you happy. When I began studying culinary arts, people said, 'Why would you want to do that?' They didn't know what was in my heart. They didn't understand my passion. I was in love with Italian cooking, and I felt I had to be true to my love.

"The truth is, if you're doing something you really love, something that makes you happy, you're going to be successful at it."

Maria Liberati is a professional chef and author of the best-selling book *The Basic Art of Italian Cooking*. For more about Maria, visit her website: www.marialiberati.com.

Creativity is inventing, experimenting,
growing, taking risks, breaking rules,
making mistakes, and having fun.
—*Mary Lou Cook, author*

IT CAN TAKE A LONG TIME FOR TALENT TO BLOSSOM

Grandma Moses was a renowned folk artist who didn't begin painting until she was in her 70s, after arthritis forced her to give up her career in embroidery. Her real name was Anna Mary Robertson Moses. She lived to be 101, producing more than 3,600 paintings in the last 30 years of her life!

Grandma Moses was discovered in 1938 by art collector Louis Caldor. He saw her paintings in a drugstore window in Hoosick Falls, New York. A year later, art dealer Otto Kallir exhibited some of her work in his New York gallery, Galerie Saint-Etienne. This exhibition catapulted her into a world she never dreamed of, much less thought she would become a part of. Collectors all over the world sought to buy her paintings. Later exhibits in Japan and Europe further spread her fame and drove up the price of her work.

Before she was "discovered," she sold her small paintings for $2 and large ones for $3. She often gave paintings to family members as thank-you gifts after her visits with them. Fast-forward to today—a 1942 painting titled *The Old Checkered House, 1862* was appraised at $60,000 in 2004. The owner had purchased the painting for $10 sometime in the 1940s.

Another of her works, *Fourth of July*, painted in honor of President

Dwight Eisenhower in the 1950s, still hangs in the White House today.

So if your busy life keeps you from expressing your creativity, it's okay. You can start when you're 70, just like Grandma Moses.

If you do things well, do them better. Be daring, be first, be different, be just.

—*Anita Roddick, founder of The Body Shop*

FROM DISSECTING FROGS
TO KISSING FROGS

When Marilyn Anderson went to college, she studied science because her mother wanted her to marry a doctor. "I met lots of doctors," Marilyn says today, "but I didn't marry any of them."

As a little girl, she had always been involved in more artsy things—performing in school plays, writing for the school newspaper, participating in social clubs. But as she got older, she put aside those creative interests to earn a BA as well as a master's degree in Biology. "After graduate school, I went to work in a lab at Hahnemann Medical School in Philadelphia, but I hated it. My boss fired me after just a couple of months, and I cried. He could see that my personality wasn't really suited to laboratory research, and we both knew he was right. It hurt my feelings, but it was one of the best things that ever happened to me."

"So, what did you do then?" I asked Marilyn.

"I got a job at the National Academy of Sciences and moved to Washington, DC. This time, my work was much more in the arena of public relations—working in information services for the biomedical organization. It was much more social.

"But over time, I began to realize that what I really loved was my life outside of work. I was performing in local and regional dinner theaters and having a ball.

"Finally, I went to my boss and told him I was leaving my job. 'What, are you quitting to get your MRS degree?' he asked. 'There's nothing better than getting married!' I told him that I was moving to New York to pursue my first love—acting. It really bothered me that he thought the only reason a woman would quit her job was to get married. That kind of thinking was typical at the time—women's career aspirations weren't taken seriously. We weren't supposed to have any serious career goals!"

"What happened when you went to New York?" I asked.

"It was amazing," she exclaimed. "A week after I got there, I was cast in a Broadway show!"

"That *is* amazing."

"But after eight performances, the show closed," she said. "That was a taste of what I was to experience many times over the years—the high of getting a great part or selling a screenplay, and the low of the show failing or the screenplay never being produced. Show business is full of ups and downs like that."

"So I've heard. So what came next for you?"

"I went to the Comic Strip, a comedy club in New York where people like Jerry Seinfeld and Eddie Murphy got their start," Marilyn said. "I liked comedy but I didn't really have an act. I could sing—not great like Streisand, of course—and I could dance okay, but I didn't have a comedy act. If I wanted to work at the Comic Strip, I needed an act.

"I went to the New York Public Library to do some research. I remembered that my father used to have a subscription to *Playboy*—somebody gave it to him as a gift every year. When it came in the mail I would always read it first, then my mom and brother would read it. Sometimes Dad never saw it at all! On the back of the centerfold photo, *Playboy* always had great jokes. So I thought I'd go through a bunch of old magazines at the library and use those jokes to build my act. But much to my dismay, all the centerfolds were missing, so the jokes were gone, too. I realized I was going to have to write my own comedy material."

I chuckled. "That's a funny story."

"What can I say?" Marilyn replied. "Life is funny. At least *my* life is funny. I got a job as a waitress at the Comic Strip and started writing comedy. I would wait tables to earn tips, and perform comedy, which paid nothing. I did some summer stock, too, and worked really hard to make it as a performer.

"Finally, in 1982, I decided that I needed to get a real job—either that, or take a vacation. I chose the vacation.

"I traveled to Los Angeles to take a break, but somehow I just never went back to New York. I vowed I was going to make it in Hollywood. I was going to act and write scripts. Everyone told me, 'Oh, you'll never get an agent. You'll never sell a script. You'll never get hired.' But I didn't listen to them. I got an agent with one of the biggest, most powerful talent agencies in the business.

"I did temp work on the side, like lots of aspiring actors and writers. One day I was assigned a temp job for one day on a TV show, *Laverne and Shirley*. At the end of the day, the producers offered me a job—to work as a secretary for them. I told them that I wasn't really a secretary, but if they would let me come to meetings and pitch ideas once in a while, I would do the secretarial work. They said okay.

"This was the last season of the show, and toward the end of my time there I pitched a story idea and they loved it. They told me to take the rest of the week off and write the script, so I did. We were all ready to go, and then the actor playing opposite Penny Marshall (Laverne) didn't show up on the set for work. It turned out that he had been killed in a car accident the night before. The show that I wrote never got produced.

"It was another one of those highs and lows of the entertainment business. It was to happen to me many times—getting a script optioned and then never having it produced.

"I wrote episodes for *Fame, Sherman Oaks,* and *Murphy Brown,* and was on the writing staff for *Carol & Company,* starring Carol Burnett. I was really getting good at writing funny. Then, one day, while I was having a quiet lunch by myself, I got an idea about frogs. I was reflecting on my dating life and suddenly the concept for a book popped into my head: *Never Kiss a Frog: A Girl's Guide to Creatures from the*

Dating Swamp. I started writing."

"I can hardly wait to hear more about these frogs," I said with a laugh.

"There's Count Frogula, who sucks you dry, the Godfrogger, the Limp Leaper, the All-Work-and-No-Play Frog, and Dr. Jekyll and Mr. Frog—to name just a few.

"I had a lot of fun writing it and putting together my book proposal. My boyfriend, Dennis, and I went to Book Expo in Chicago in 2001 to shop the proposal around. I landed an agent, who promptly took my proposal to the Frankfurt Book Fair a few months later and sold the book to publishers in Spain and Germany. It was hysterical—I hadn't even finished writing the book and it got sold into two foreign languages! I had planned on getting an illustrator, but the Spanish publisher said she liked the informal doodles in the proposal and insisted that I illustrate the book myself. Suddenly I am not only an author, I'm an illustrator."

"Sounds like you're willing and able to jump from one lily pad to another pretty easily," I teased Marilyn.

"Wait, there's more," she said. "When my book finally got published in the US, I suddenly discovered that people considered me a dating expert. I got hired to be the flirting and kissing expert on the TV show *Extreme Makeover.* I've done hundreds of radio and TV shows. You know what's really funny? I've been on TV more as a book author than I ever was when I was an actress."

"What a great story!"

"It goes on," Marilyn continued. "Just last year, a producer called me about an idea that I first had twenty-five years ago. I had pitched it to her ten years ago. Last year, out of the blue, she calls and asks, 'Is that story still available? I think I can sell it.' So within a few short months she sold the story, I wrote the screenplay, the movie was produced, and it aired on television."

"Your life is just full of surprises, isn't it?"

"Yup," Marilyn replied. "As I think back on my life I see this odd kind of continuity. I didn't like dissecting frogs in a lab, but I love dissecting and analyzing frogs in the world of dating."

I laughed. "You're too funny. So what advice would you give others about being true to themselves and finding their life's passion? Seriously, now."

"I would tell people that you never know what one thing will take you where you want to go. It's never the thing you think it will be. For instance, I have pitched and sold more screenplays through connections I made at parties than I ever have working with an agent.

"Second, I would advise people to never say no. If you say yes you never know where it will take you. Let the world in. Say yes when opportunities present themselves. You might be in for a wonderful surprise—better than anything you could have ever planned."

To learn more about Marilyn Anderson and her frogs, visit her "webbed" site: www.neverkissafrog.com.

I believe talent is like electricity. We do not understand electricity. We use it. Electricity makes no judgment. You can plug into it, and light up a lamp, keep a heart pump going, light a cathedral, or you can electrocute a person with it.... I think talent is like that. I believe every person is born with a talent.

—Maya Angelou, *poet, author, actress, university professor*

When I stand before God at the end of my life, I would hope that I would not have a single bit of talent left, and could say: I used everything you gave me.

—*Erma Bombeck, writer, humorist*

NEVER-TOO-LATE TIPS FOR BECOMING CREATIVE

1.
Expand your definition of "creative." It's much more than music and fine art. Your creativity might be cooking, fashion, writing, decorating your home, gardening, or flower arranging, and much, much more. Express your creativity in your own unique way.

2.
Take time to stimulate your imagination with occasional "creativity days." Visit museums; go to author events at local bookstores; take walks in nature; browse through beautiful coffee-table books; go to a concert or theater performance.

3.
Make a list of the creative people you most admire. Let their creativity stimulate yours.

4.
Give yourself permission to make "bad art" in the beginning. Getting good at any art form takes lots of practice, with many "mistakes" along the way. Let go of perfectionism.

5.
Enjoy the process of discovering and getting to know your muse. Let your intuition and imagination guide you.
Have fun!

CHAPTER 5

IT'S NEVER TOO LATE TO GATHER WEALTH

Every morning I get up and look at Forbes' list of the richest people in America. If I'm not there, I go to work.

—Robert Orben,
magician and comedy writer

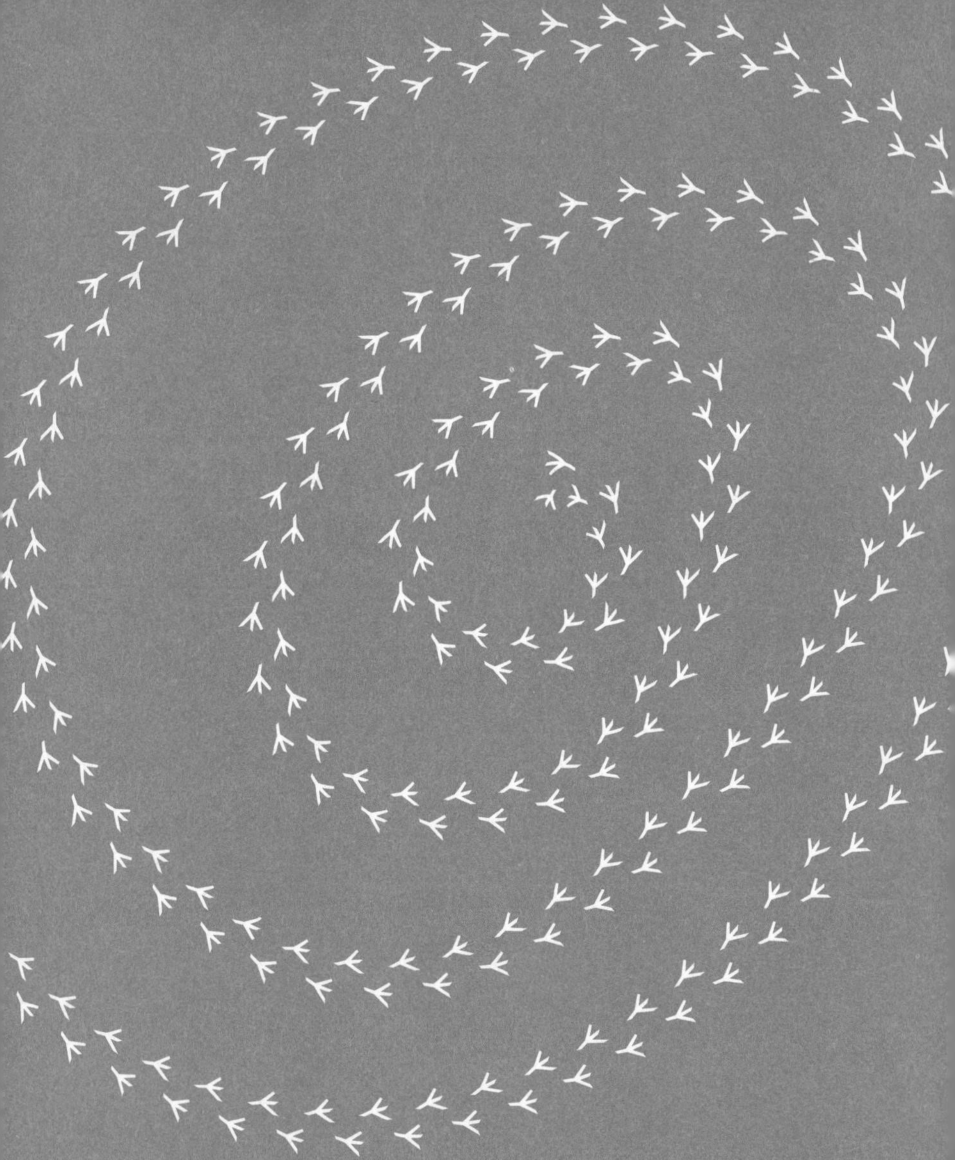

Recently I was doing some research on the Internet, looking for famous quotes about money. It was fascinating to see how many smart, famous people throughout history have commented on money. What was even more fascinating was how extreme their comments were. Many well-respected people have nothing but condemnation for money—they think it is a corrupting influence on individuals and society. But other well-respected people have only positive things to say about money—they rank it right up there with oxygen in terms of importance. So, who's right?

Well, I'm a positive, upbeat person, so I'm going with the famous folks who think money is a good thing—a powerful tool to be used for social and individual improvement. I think that making money is a creative act—it's stimulating, fun, and challenges my resourcefulness and imagination. I like money—it can buy me freedom from mundane tasks I don't like to do. I love to give money away to help people and support worthwhile causes like animal rescue and disaster relief.

It's never too late to make money—lots of money, if you're so inclined. The key factor in whether you will ever do so or not is your beliefs and attitudes about money. So start there. If you harbor the notion that money is dirty, evil, or corrupting, forget trying to get rich—your beliefs will keep you from accumulating substantial wealth. If you think that money is useful, helpful, and a powerful influence to be used for good, then go for it—gather as much wealth as your attention, energy, and commitment can produce.

Just remember to do everything you can to enjoy the *making* of money as much as you enjoy the having of it. Have fun with the process!

BECOMING A MONEY MAGNET

Chellie Campbell is a money magnet—people just love to give her money. She is a successful author who writes popular books about money; she lives in a million-dollar house in an upscale section of Los Angeles; she coaches an international team of trainers who teach her Financial Stress Reduction® classes; she drives a luxury import car; she takes cruises whenever she feels like it; and she plays medium-stakes poker for fun and for money. At midlife, Chellie is living the life of her dreams.

But that wasn't always the case. Chellie's first career choice was actress. She studied acting in high school and college, spent years paying her dues in heartless Hollywood, and worked hard to be "discovered" in order to become a star.

While supporting herself with clerical work between auditions, she developed bookkeeping skills. After years of working for others, she bought the bookkeeping business she worked for and built it into a successful operation with almost half a million dollars in yearly revenues.

But that all came crashing down when she lost her biggest client, who had accounted for 75 percent of Chellie's income. She had 12 employees at the time, working in a brand-new office space she had leased. "I was absolutely strapped for cash, having been left with many financial obligations and no current means of paying for them," she explained. "I borrowed fifty thousand dollars on credit cards."

"Yikes!" I exclaimed when Chellie told me that.

"Wait, it gets worse," she said. "Five years later, I had faithfully paid the minimum balances every month, but over that time I had developed the bad habit of using credit cards whenever cash flow dipped. Compound interest ate me alive. By this time, my fifty thousand dollars debt had grown to eighty thousand dollars. Then my chief bookkeeper quit and went into business for herself, taking a lot of my clients with her. My ex-business partners were pressuring me to pay them for the purchase of the company.

"I tried to sell the condo I had purchased at the top of the real estate market in 1987, but its value had plummeted and I now owed thirty thousand dollars more than it was worth. It didn't really matter, because the market had gotten so soft that I couldn't find a buyer at any price. I couldn't keep up with my regular bills, much less my debts. My financial spiral downward was matched by my emotional spiral into despair. Long story short, I ended up in bankruptcy."

I winced. "Ouch."

"Ouch, indeed," Chellie said.

"So, how did you get from the financial and emotional bottom, where you were, to where you are today?" I asked her.

"I won't bore you will all the painful details," she replied. "But here's what I learned, in a nutshell. There are three ways to be successful in having the standard of living you want: One, earn more. Two, spend less. Three, find another way to have what you want. My rags-to-riches recovery entails doing all three."

"I understand the first two," I told her, "but tell me more about the third item."

"Okay," she said. "In those dark days of my bankruptcy, I also lost my condo to foreclosure. It was a humiliating personal disaster.

"One Friday night, I was playing cards with several girlfriends. They all knew I was going through a hard time and one of them turned to me and asked, 'Where are you going to live now?' I said, 'I don't know.' She thought about it a minute and then said, 'Perhaps you could move in here with Shelley.' Shelley looked up from her cards and said, 'Sure, you can move in with me. Since my divorce, it's just me living in this big house. There's plenty of room for you and your cat.'

"So I moved into Shelley's gorgeous two-story, three-bedroom, three-bath, three-thousand-square-foot home on a lovely hillside in Brentwood, an upscale part of Los Angeles. Her furniture was wonderful, her art to my taste, and the earth-tone interior colors looked made-to-order for me. It was the most beautiful—and most expensive—home I had ever lived in. Shelley and I got along great, and I enjoyed having a roommate after living alone for so many years. The rent? A whopping two hundred dollars per month."

"Wow, that's great!"

"You bet it's great," Chellie said. "It was so great that it's been fifteen years and I'm still living there. My rent is closer to a thousand dollars a month, but it's still a good deal. I get to live in this wonderful home without having to own it. No headaches with roof repairs or water heaters or property tax."

"You still like having a roommate?"

"Better than ever. Shelley and I have become great friends. We both like to play poker; we enjoy going on cruises; and our personalities and lifestyles are compatible. She lets me use the living room to teach my Financial Stress Reduction® classes, and I run my business out of the third bedroom. Shelley is at work all day, so I have the whole house to myself. We lead our independent lives, but we can choose when we want to hang out together.

"Neither of us plans to marry again—we've both been through painful divorces. So as far as I can tell, we'll share this house for many years."

"That's a great story."

"The point is, you don't have to *be* rich to *live* rich," Chellie said. "I found another way to have what I want—which is a lovely home. And in this case, it also enabled me to spend less while I earned more. Living in Shelley's house gave me a great place to live while I regrouped and reorganized my life.

"I don't have the bookkeeping business anymore. Instead, I taught Financial Stress Reduction® classes for many years, and now I train other people to teach them, while I coach, support, and mentor them. I have a six-figure income, lots of money socked away in investments, and plenty of time to travel, play poker, and enjoy my friends and family."

"You're wealthy in more ways than one."

"Yes—and not a day goes by that I don't thank God for the many blessings I have in my life. I am rich in joy, happiness, good friends, a business that I love, and a wonderful place to live. I'm sixty years old and happier than I've ever been!"

"Chellie, you've gone from bankruptcy to huge financial success," I said. "What advice would you give others who might be struggling with career or money issues today?"

Chellie thought for a minute and then said, "You take a long, cold look at what you were doing that doesn't belong in your world anymore. For instance, I was done with bookkeeping but I had to practically destroy my business before I could leave it. It had become a security blanket, just like a job. What I really loved was the speaking and workshops that I had been doing. But fear of financial insecurity kept me trapped until I lost everything anyway.

"From destitution, there was no place to go but up. After hitting bottom, I thought I might as well go for what I really wanted. I didn't know if I could make a living teaching workshops or not, but the alternatives, like getting a job, were just too distasteful to me—so I decided I would make this work or die trying.

"Here's what I tell my workshop participants: When you're Dorothy and your goal is the Emerald City, you are willing to take any path to get there. Determination is like an iron fist in your gut. You will not be dissuaded from your dream because there's a witch on the road, or flying monkeys overhead, or a forbidding guard between you and the Emerald City. You will never be one of those small-minded people who are content to stay forever in Munchkinland. You must be determined to get to the Emerald City or die trying. That's what it takes to be successful."

For more about Chellie Campbell and her Financial Stress Reduction® workshops, see her website: www.chellie.com.

From birth to age 18, a girl needs good parents,
from 18 to 35 she needs good looks,
from 35 to 55 she needs a good personality,
and from 55 on she needs cash.

—*Sophie Tucker, jazz singer*

Being rich is having money;
being wealthy is having time.

—*Margaret Bonanno,*
Star Trek *novelist*

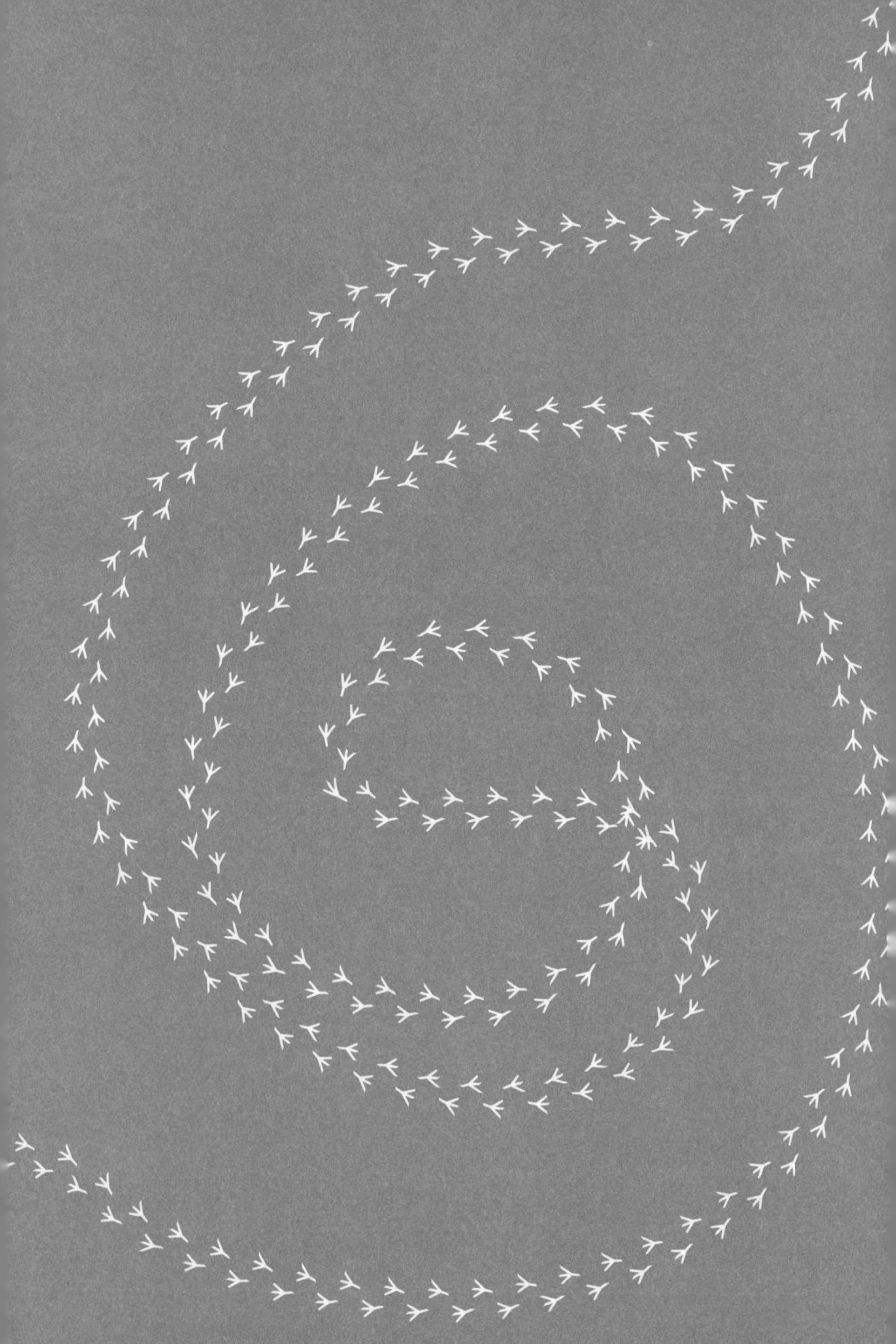

IT'S NEVER TOO LATE TO
HAVE MONEY...

MAKE it.
OWN it.
NEVER IGNORE it.
ENJOY it.
YAK about it.

Money isn't everything—but it ranks right up there
with oxygen.

—Rita Davenport, comedian

TOP GUN

Bob Smith is a great example of someone who has "the right stuff." He's confident but not arrogant, smart but not an egghead, aggressive but not reckless, and he knows his strengths as well as his limits. He's now 75 and eager to share what he knows about learning and earning.

"The first twenty years of my adult life were pretty typical for a married man in the nineteen-fifties and sixties," Bob began his story. "I was an Air Force officer and fighter pilot, while my wife was a traditional wife and mother who raised our two kids and served as a support system for me. We were married for twenty-plus years.

"I retired from the service in 1974, at age forty. I was a lieutenant colonel making twenty-seven thousand dollars at the time. I started an investment brokerage business and within seventeen months I made my first million."

"That's amazing," I said. "How did you do that?"

"I started early. For the previous sixteen years, I'd been educating myself and preparing myself for the future. I sold investments on a part-time basis wherever I went. I opened little branch offices wherever I was stationed in the Air Force. There is no substitute for experience and training when you're preparing for a career change down the line.

"My wife and I divorced and we split everything fifty/fifty. She got all the assets and I got all the debt. But I didn't mind giving her everything—she had been a wonderful support system for me while I was building my career, and I figured she had earned everything I gave her. But she did not get my education or my earning potential—those were mine. And I knew I could use them to build a new life for myself."

"That's very generous, as well as optimistic."

"I mean every word of it," Bob said. "I don't begrudge her a thing. When I left my marriage I was paying mortgages on two houses, alimony to my wife, three college tuitions—my wife and both my kids were in college—and child support for my son who was still living at home.

"Then, in 1977, the brokerage house I was working with was put out of business and I had to start all over again. I was forty-three years old and pretty much broke, after I finished paying all my obligations. At one point, I even had to borrow money from my ex-wife to pay her alimony and child support! But she knew I would pay it back, with interest."

"And did you?"

"You bet. I established myself with a new brokerage house and set up my own business all over again. I took three hundred dollars and rented three small rooms. The first month, I made ten thousand dollars, so I hired a part-time secretary and a couple of salesmen. The next month, I made another ten thousand dollars, so I put the secretary on full-time and hired a couple more salesmen. I trained all my own people. I kept expanding gradually like that, using the money I made to plow back into the business, hiring and training more people and renting more space. Over the years, I kept building, investing, hiring, and training, until finally I became one of the larger high-end tax planning and investment planning brokerage firms on the East Coast."

"That's remarkable. How did you do it?"

"Simple," Bob answered. "I had no debt to service and I had the knowledge I needed. I never borrowed money to expand—I grew the business slowly and steadily, spending only what was coming in the door. And I'd spent sixteen to eighteen years getting the training and education I needed. I had picked up a master's degree at Berkeley while I was still in the Air Force. I knew what I wanted to do when I retired, so I started preparing myself years in advance.

"I had learned from some great people over the years. I recall, back in 1958, my first sales manager told me, 'Bob, do you know why so many people want to get rich quick? Because they don't know how to get rich slow.' And that's what I was really good at, helping my clients to get rich slow. I'm patient. I take the long view of investing. When my wife and I split up, we had some investments that were very aggressive and very risky. She didn't want any part of them, so I got them in the divorce. Later on, they paid off very nicely."

"How do you know what investments to buy?"

"My specialty is doing due diligence," Bob replied. "I look at cash flow, profit potential, growth potential, and competitive businesses. I need to get my arms around a business and fully understand it before I'm willing to invest. If I can't get my arms around it, I don't buy into it. As a former colleague of mine used to say, 'No deal is so good that you can't walk away from it.'

"Second, I look for investment opportunities that are small enough that the big guys don't want to bother with them. In other words, I go where there isn't a lot of competition. I call it my Puddle Theory: I make a nice living in small puddles where the big guys don't want to swim. I always tell my clients, 'Don't get greedy. We can do quite well being medium-sized fish in small puddles—we don't need to go out in the ocean with the sharks.'

"Look, the best way to make money is to have a 'widget'—you either make it or service it. Your widget is something that you know more about than anyone else. You're the expert—you're the go-to guy or gal when someone wants that particular widget. So my widget is being an expert in small puddle investments.

"My third principle of success is making sure that every deal is win–win–win. I invest in deals so that my clients win, I win, and the business we invest in wins.

"There are some people out there who are looking for how they can screw other people—they think win–lose. In my opinion, they deserve to lose. And if you look around today, with all the financial disasters all over the place, that's what you're seeing. In the fifty years I've been doing this, almost everyone who's worked or invested with me has made money, and the handful of deals that went bad didn't go bad because of anything I did. Nobody got burned. Every once in a while a deal doesn't pay off, even though you did due diligence and made good decisions. That's part of the game. But all of my clients—all of them—would tell you that I did my very best to make a fair return on their investments."

"Are you still running your brokerage business?"

"Heavens, no!" Bob laughed. "I retired in 1985 at age fifty-one. I was a multimillionaire by then and wanted to relax and enjoy my money. I'm an avid sportsman and love to travel, ski, golf, and enjoy water sports. I remarried some years ago and my wife, Diane, and I have a wonderful life together here in Henderson, Nevada. We have a second home in Illinois, where her family lives, and we make time to enjoy kids, grandkids, and others.

"I still handle my own investments, of course. I love making money—it's just nice that I don't have to do it for a living anymore. I met all my obligations to my first wife and kids, and I feel good about that. I am able to take care of my second wife so that she could retire and travel with me. What can I say? Life is good."

"You've included lots of good advice in your story," I said. "Any final words of advice you'd offer?"

"I'd just emphasize what I said earlier," Bob replied. "You need to get smart—get the training and education you need if you want to start a successful career or business later in life. Also, live within your means. Don't take on debt to start something new. Start small and build. Develop patience and perseverance so that you can get rich slowly."

Money is better than poverty, if only for financial reasons.

—Woody Allen, filmmaker

FINGER-LICKIN' TASTY SUCCESS

The story of Colonel Sanders and his Kentucky Fried Chicken has long been one of my favorite stories of financial success in later life.

In 1930, at age 40, Harland "Colonel" Sanders started cooking for people who stopped at his service station in Corbin, Kentucky. He had been cooking since he was a child—his father died when he was just five, and his mother had to work to support the family. Young Harland dropped out of school in seventh grade and ran away from home after his mother remarried a man who beat him. In his young life he worked a variety of jobs, including insurance salesman, farmer, railroad fireman, steamboat driver, and Army soldier.

At his service station, Sanders didn't have an actual restaurant, so he served meals in his living quarters. As word of his tasty food got around and his popularity increased, Sanders needed to find a larger place to feed his customers, so he moved to a motel with a 142-seat restaurant. He spent the next decade refining and perfecting his special fried chicken recipe.

The Colonel didn't franchise his chicken business until 1955, when construction of a nearby interstate freeway significantly reduced the number of customers frequenting his restaurant. He was 65 at the time, and used $105 from his first Social Security check to start his franchise business.

Nine years later, in 1964, Colonel Sanders sold his American franchise operation for $2 million. Now, that's not chicken feed!

When I was young, I thought that money was the most important thing in life; now that I am old, I know that it is.

—*Oscar Wilde, playwright*

Early to bed and early to rise—till you get enough money to do otherwise.

—*Peter's Almanac*

MONEY EQUALS FREEDOM

My friend Kate Higgens is one of the smartest people I know when it comes to money. Trained as a social worker (not a lucrative profession, by a long shot), she did not marry money nor did she inherit it. Yet she lives in a multimillion-dollar beachfront Florida home, just steps from the soft sand and shimmering water. She has all the clothes, jewelry, art, cars, and nice things anyone could ever want—and the time to enjoy them. And best of all, she shares her wealth—donating tens of thousands of dollars to animal rescue groups and organizations taking care of disadvantaged kids. How did she achieve such financial success, starting off as a social worker?

I asked Kate if she would share what she had learned about money over the years, so others might learn from her experience.

"Money is like a hammer," Kate told me. "It's a tool. You can use it to build something, or you can use it to destroy something. The hammer is neutral—and so is money. How you use it is what makes the difference in your life.

"When I was a little girl, my mother had an old desk. On either side, she had two love letter boxes. One was called her 'Pony Fund' and the other was her 'Running Away Fund.' Was she really planning on running away from Dad and us kids? I don't know. She never left, so I suppose she just liked having the *option* to run away if she chose to. She never bought the pony, either, but she kept the dream alive by saving for it."

"What did you learn from your mom's savings habits?" I asked Kate.

"I learned that these were funds with which you could make stuff happen," she answered. "Money can buy you something you want, and money can buy you an escape from an unhappy situation. Money is freedom—to buy what you want and to live as you want."

"So, what was your next big lesson about money?"

"Well, I was just out of college with my degree in social work," Kate said. "I was making five thousand dollars a year and just getting by. Then one day my old car broke down, and I had a hard time scraping together the money to repair it. It suddenly became clear to me that I needed to have a fund for 'Life Happens'—for solving unforeseen problems."

"What came next?"

"When I was thirty, I left regular employment—I really didn't have the temperament to work for others. I didn't like the way the game was played; I wanted to make up my own game and make my own rules.

"So I realized that, from then on, I really did have to take care of myself—no one was going to plan my career or make sure that I could retire someday. I asked some smart people, 'How much money do I need by the time I retire?' Their estimate was about a million dollars, to live off the interest dividends. So that became my goal, and I started from there.

"Of course, I realize there was no way a social worker could ever save a million dollars, no matter how long I worked or how frugal I was. The only solution was to make my money work for me. I started learning about investments and studying how money works."

"What did you learn?"

"Well, I had one more painful lesson to learn before the happy lessons started," Kate said. "When I first started earning money as a self-employed person, I was shocked to discover that it wasn't all mine to keep. The government wanted a third of it in taxes. I was devastated.

It felt like I had earned my money and now someone wanted to take a big chunk of it away from me. You see, previously, when I had been employed by someone else, the taxes were taken out before I ever got my pay, so I never missed it. But now, I had to pay my own taxes and I missed the money a lot. I had to learn: How much of the money I earn is really mine to keep?

"So I set up three accounts: one-third of my money for taxes, one-third for my Freedom Fund, and one-third to live on. Then I organized my life around what I could afford—what I could get for that one-third that was really mine to spend."

"How did you do that?"

"I learned several important, helpful, practical things about money:

1. You don't have to pay cash for everything—you can barter. For instance, during my first year in Florida, I lived with two very busy people in their lovely home. I cooked dinner for them every night and walked their dog, in exchange for free rent and board. I had no money coming in at that time, but I also had no money going out—and I was living very well.

2. I learned about all the things that have no value after a certain point in time—like hotel rooms and theater tickets. If I arrive at a hotel late in the evening, I can often get a room at half price because they know that no one else is coming so late, and the room has no value to them if it sits empty. It's the same with theater tickets: after the curtain goes up, any unsold tickets are worthless. So I go to the theater half an hour before curtain time and see if I can get tickets at a reduced price. Often I can. If not, then I have a Plan B in place, and I go walk on the beach instead. So I never feel deprived or disappointed.

3. I learned how to ASK and to NEGOTIATE. For instance, if I knew a sale was coming up soon, I might go to the store and pick out what I wanted, then ask if I could have the sale price early. Often, that answer was yes because the clerk knew a sale price today was better than the chance that I wouldn't come back during the actual sale.

4. I developed internal flexibility. For example, I can go to my favorite restaurant and have a wonderful meal at five P.M. that would cost twice as much two hours later. I can go to the movies in the afternoon and see the same movie that would cost double a few hours later. I usually get what I want if I'm not attached to when I get it.

5. I learned the difference between wants and needs. Wants are preferences—what movie to go to, where to eat, et cetera; needs are essential for survival—like oxygen, water, and food. For instance, I might *want* my own house, but I didn't really *need* a whole house all to myself—I just needed my own space, some privacy, and quiet. When I recognized the difference between wants and needs, I teamed up with two other women, and together we bought a five-bedroom home in Palm Beach. We ended up sharing that home for the next fourteen years, and for six hundred and fifty dollars a month I lived in a gorgeous place with stunning ocean views. I had one bedroom to sleep in and another bedroom for my office—my housemates went to work each day so I had the place to myself. We all had a better lifestyle together than any of us could have had alone.

"In short, I always kept my priorities in mind—I wanted freedom more than I wanted things—so I acted accordingly. *Freedom* became as concrete to me as a new car might be to someone else. I learned to be creative and resourceful, and got a kick out of saving. I never felt deprived. I was buying what mattered most to me."

"Those are all great lessons about saving money," I said. "Then how did you put your money to work for you?"

"I had to learn lessons on how to do that, too," she replied. "I had my million-dollar goal and needed to find out how to use my Freedom Fund to get there.

"I studied the stock market and started investing. I did that for years. A therapist friend of mine and I both learned all we could about companies and stocks and how to pick good investments. The two of us learned together and we both got good at it. Then he got much better at it than I was, so I decided to let him invest my money, too. I knew him, trusted him, and he had a proven track record.

"I learned about defined benefit programs—SEP IRAs and things like that. I put my Freedom Fund money in those tax-deferred buckets and let it grow. I learned about the power of compounding—that money can grow pretty fast if you let it be and don't touch it.

"Every once in a while I'd buy a piece of real estate, if it was a good price and I knew I could fix it up and sell it later at a profit. I did that two or three times. But real estate wasn't really my thing—I just did it when it was convenient and easy."

"That's all great advice, Kate. Thanks for sharing so much with me. I have just one more question: What if someone is starting late in learning to manage their money?"

"There's no such thing as late," Kate replied. "People need to give up that notion of 'It's too late, so I might as well do nothing.' You can always do *something,* even if you can't do *everything.* Start where you are.

"For instance, defined benefit programs have a makeup clause which says that after a certain age, you can put unlimited amounts of your money in, tax-free, and let it work for you until you retire. That's a great way to play catch-up and make your money work for you.

"Wherever you are in your life is a fine place to start. Spend less than you make. Pay cash—don't use credit cards. Learn to negotiate and barter. Start your Freedom Fund *today!* Make it fun and make it a game. Take time to learn how money works—then put your money to work."

"Thanks, Kate," I said as I hugged her. "I needed that."

We both laughed, then headed out the door for a matinee movie and an early-bird dinner.

Money, if it does not bring you
happiness, will at least help
you to be miserable
in comfort.

—*Lord Mancroft,*
British politician

I'm tired of Love;
I'm still more tired of Rhyme.
But Money gives me pleasure
all the time.

—*Hilaire Belloc,*
French-born British poet,
author, and orator

NEVER-TOO-LATE TIPS FOR
GATHERING WEALTH

1.

Start where you are. There is no such thing as "too late" to get good with money. The important thing is that you start.

2.

Learn about money and how it works. Read a handful of good books about money. Attend financial seminars and workshops. Seek out people whose advice you trust.

3.

Make an accurate assessment of your tolerance for risk. Honor it. Don't let others push you into something that doesn't feel right for you.

4.

Start a Freedom Fund.

5.

Cut up your credit cards. Learn to live below your means so that you can save some for the future. Live on a cash-only basis, except for secured debt like houses and cars.

CHAPTER 6

IT'S NEVER TOO LATE TO BECOME ATHLETIC

Champions aren't made in the gyms. Champions are made
from something they have deep inside them—
a desire, a dream, a vision.

—*Muhammad Ali, world heavyweight boxing champion*

The best thing I ever did to become more athletic was to adopt a dog. What does a dog have to do with fitness? I'll tell you.

Seven years ago, I woke up one morning and thought to myself, *Heck, I can't find a husband—I'm going to get a dog*. I'd never had a dog before; I'd always been a cat person. (I owned seven cats at that point.) But I decided that I wanted to have the experience of a dog sometime in my life, and this was as good a time as any.

I began my search of the local animal shelters and contacted rescue groups. One day, on a visit to a nearby city shelter, I found a darling golden puppy—mixed breed, Chow and Pekingese. She was a funny-looking mutt, with a Chow face and black tongue, Peke underbite and short fluffy ears, and the thickest, softest, blonde fur you could imagine. It was love at first sight—at least for me. She had a funny face, like funny girl Fanny Brice, so I named her Fannie.

The pup was just five months old and had no bad habits, thank goodness. I decided that if I was going to be a dog owner, I wanted to be a good one, so I made a commitment to take her on a long walk every morning. I live on top of a small mountain and began walking three miles up and down the mountain each day.

Before the dog arrived in my life, I had a million excuses for not walking in the morning. *It's too cold. It's too hot. Oops, I'm running late; can't walk today. I'm tired; I'll walk tomorrow.* And many more. But Fannie changed all that. She has to go outdoors to pee, so skipping my morning walk was no longer an option. And I figured as long as we had to go out, we might as well make it a good, long walk. I'm already dressed and out the door, might as well keep going.

After the first few months, I noticed I was slimming down, though not losing weight. Muscle weighs more than fat, so my weight wasn't changing but the fat weight was shifting to muscle weight. My legs toned up and my butt got firmer. I felt better, too, starting my day with my heart pumping and endorphins humming through my body. I was pleased with the changes.

For seven years now, I wake up each morning to Fannie's eager face and wagging tail. As I get out of bed and reach for my sweats and shoes, she runs to the door and waits for me. She never scolds if I'm late—she's happy to go no matter what time it is. She never barks orders at me—she just trots along, stopping here and there to check her pee-mail left by other dogs. She leads the way with her perky tail held high like a drum majorette's baton.

I now refer to Fannie as my little personal trainer. She inspires me; she leads me; she encourages me. She is my partner in fitness. If you're looking for an easy way to become more athletic, consider adopting a great dog.

GOING TO NEW HEIGHTS

December 31, 2000, was an important day for Arnold Chanin and his wife, Raine—it was the day they went on their first hike. Arnie was 66 and Raine was 61—neither was particularly athletic. "We had started walking a few months earlier, but it was just going for short walks in our neighborhood or in the hills behind our home," Arnie told me. "We live in Encino, California, a suburb of Los Angeles, and our house backs up to the Santa Monica Mountains. We used to take casual strolls just for fresh air and a little relaxation.

"I'm not sure why we decided to change from walking to hiking—it was just for the great scenery, as I recall. I'm a physician and I've been going to the gym every morning for years, and that was always enough for me. Deciding to hike had nothing to do with my health, or Raine's either. We just thought it might be fun. So on New Years' Eve day, we went on a short hike in Temescal Canyon—it was just a couple of hours.

"We enjoyed that year-end hike and decided to go on more hikes in the New Year. We hiked three or four miles—nothing major. We bought a book about hiking—*One Hundred Hikes in the Los Angeles Area*—and gradually worked our way through the book.

"Then we got a bit bored and decided to try hiking in the nearby

San Gabriel Mountains. Which were very different from what we were used to."

"How so?" I asked.

"Well, the San Gabriels are granite, not sandstone like the Santa Monicas," Arnie answered. "The tree leaves change with the seasons, and there are waterfalls. The mountains are much bigger, too. Hiking in the San Gabriel Mountains was dramatically different from what we'd been doing up to that point.

"I noticed that our motivation had changed along with our mountains. Early on, we just took short hikes for fun. We got good at it so we started to get serious. We bought equipment—good boots, hats, a knife, backpacks, a little cookstove, and other things. We spent time in the local sporting goods store, talking to the hiking experts and educating ourselves. We approached hiking from a more technical perspective, spending all week planning and preparing for the next weekend's hike. We bought more books on hiking, which I devoured, while Raine prepared food for our outings."

"Sounds like you two really immersed yourself in the sport."

"We got addicted," Arnie said. "Hiking gave us a real high—not just the hike itself, but all the preparation and planning we put into it. The endorphins produced in the activity were the ultimate high—better than any drug. The ecstasy lasts all day."

"Really?"

"Oh, yes. My wife and I are both very intense people and so no surprise that we'd get compulsive about hiking. By the end of 2001, we were hiking seven, eight, nine hours in the San Gabriel Mountains. We would start out very early in the morning and not come out of the mountains until sundown. Raine would have food packed for us—a mix of half coffee/half hot chocolate, string cheese, peanut butter and jelly sandwiches, and stuff like that.

"We also took whole weekends and drove to places like Ojai, Idyllwild, and Santa Barbara, where we'd spend three days hiking. They were day trips—we'd do one on Friday, a second on Saturday, and a third on Sunday. It was a wonderful way to enjoy Southern California."

"Did you ever go hiking anywhere outside of California?"

"Oh, yes," Arnie replied. "I used to go to the Sitka Island Institute Writers Conference and the Sitka Music Festival up in Alaska—I went for several years in a row by myself. In summer 2001, I encouraged Raine to come with me. 'We can go hiking up there,' I told her. So we flew to Sitka and hiked every day instead of going to conference sessions. The mountains were a little distance away, so we rented bikes, rode to our hiking destination, did our hike, then rode back to the hotel. In the evenings we attended author readings and chamber music concerts, which were also part of the writers conference.

"It was fabulous! The hiking, the concerts, the author readings, and the biking. Raine didn't really know how to handle the gears on a bike back then so I had to hold up my fingers to signal her which gear to use. But she was a good sport, and we realized that we liked the biking part of our adventure, too.

"So when we came back home, we started biking as well as hiking. We used old bikes at first, and rode locally. But over time we got good at it—just like we did with the hiking—and took it more seriously, buying good bikes."

"All this and you're both in your sixties."

"Actually," Arnie said, "I am seventy-four and Raine is sixty-nine, and we're still going strong. We bike all the time now, probably seventy miles each week—thirty miles on Friday and maybe forty miles on Sunday. We take it easy on Saturdays."

"And the hiking?"

"We're not doing much if any hiking now. Biking has become our new love. But we might go back to it, who knows?

"We've had some amazing experiences hiking in Alaska, the Sierras, in Yosemite, and other places. We've hiked up ten thousand feet, twelve thousand feet, gotten close to the summit of some major peaks. It's hard to describe the experience of being up so high. You're up above everything—above the waterfalls, above the forests, above the granite mountains. Looking down on the valleys below is like being literally on top of the world.

"I recall one hike we took out of Independence, California, up to Kearsarge Pass. We hiked past five alpine lakes to the top of jagged peaks, and when we got to the top, we looked down the other side to see the world as it must have looked thousands, millions of years ago—spectacular pristine beauty. It's a spiritual experience. The clouds are rolling by, the rains come and go, and I swear it feels like you could reach up and touch God."

"No wonder you loved it so much."

"Words can't even describe how moving, how beautiful, how powerful the experience is," Arnie said softly.

We both fell silent for a few moments.

"If other people wanted to have that kind of experience, what advice would you give them?" I asked.

"Taking up a new activity is like starting anything," he replied. "Start simple. Start small. You can begin by just taking short walks—in your neighborhood, in the local park, at the beach, at a lake, wherever you would enjoy the sights and smells. If you like it, then do more.

"The next step is to educate yourself. Buy a book and learn more about the sport or activity. Talk to the experts at your local store—there are plenty of stores devoted solely to hiking and/or biking.

"Make sure you have the right shoes—shoes are really important for both hiking and biking. You don't want to head off hiking in tennis shoes. You need to wear the right clothes, too—learn to dress in layers. As you get more serious, you would want to invest in a few basics—a good hat to protect your skin from the sun and wind, a good backpack to carry the supplies you'll need, a decent knife, a compass, and a few other things. My wife and I use walkie-talkies because cell phones often don't work where we hike and bike."

"Any other advice you'd add?"

"Don't go alone. Find a partner to hike or bike with. Or get a small group to go with. Raine and I don't like going with big groups, but you definitely don't want to do this alone. It's not safe, and it's not as fun, either. What has made this late-life adventure so wonderful for us is that we do it together. We're a team. It has enriched our marriage, as well as enriching each of us individually."

"Final question," I said. "Any regrets?"

Arnie smiled. "My only regret is that we didn't start doing this in our forties. But hey, you start when you start and it's never too late. The only real regret would be never to start at all."

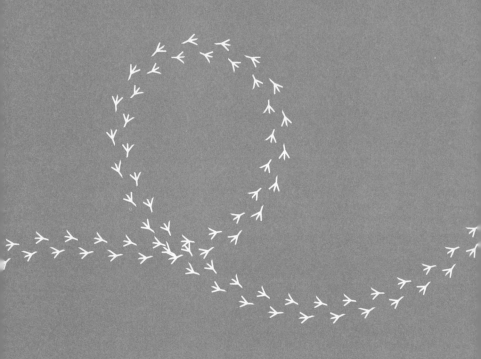

Many men go fishing all of their lives without
knowing that it is not fish they are after.

—Henry David Thoreau,
naturalist, author, philosopher

IT'S NEVER TOO LATE TO
BE A JOCK...

JUST do it.
OFF you go!
CULTIVATE active habits.
KICK into high gear.

When I step onto the court, I don't have to think about anything. If I have a problem off the court, I find that after I play, my mind is clearer and I can come up with a better solution. It's like therapy. It relaxes me and allows me to solve problems.

—*Michael Jordan, basketball star*

MIDLIFE JOCK

Marianne Callum is the last person you'd expect to turn into a midlife jock. "I absolutely hated sports when I was younger and was really bad at them. I was clumsy, overweight, and always the last one picked for teams.

"Even as an adult, I'd prefer sitting to anything else. My whole life, I've been a woman who lived in her head, not her body. I've always worked in office jobs, love to read and daydream, and pretty much ignore my body."

"So what changed?" I asked her.

"It wasn't anything dramatic," Marianne replied. "There wasn't some watershed event that changed me. It was more subtle and gradual than that—starting when I was fifty-seven. Perhaps it was increased consciousness of aging; maybe it was heightened health concerns as I saw my husband develop high blood pressure and other friends develop physical problems, too. I thought about getting older, and I've always sworn that when I'm in the crank-up bed in the nursing home thinking back on my life I want to have as few regrets as possible. I didn't want to be there saying, 'I should have exercised.'

"So one day I just decided to take a little walk in the morning before I went to work. I'm a morning person anyway, so it wasn't a big deal to get up a little earlier and begin my day with a short walk. Over time, my walks got longer. I remember how proud I was when I walked a whole mile—that was a big deal for me. It had taken me about two months to build up to that distance."

"Did you walk by yourself or did you have a walking buddy?"

"I started by walking alone," Marianne said. "I realized that I really enjoyed the morning quiet time and solitude. At the time, our son was still at home, and between my family and my work, the only time I had to myself was my morning walk. I really relished it.

"I enjoy the early morning. I love the sights and sounds of the world waking up. In winter, it's still dark when I walk, but I head into the hills around where I live and it's pretty safe there. Once, I was out for my walk in the predawn hours, and as I rounded a corner I came face-to-face with a magnificent stag. It was totally unexpected and wonderful. He and I both just stood there for a few moments, looking at each other, silently wondering, *What are* you *doing here?*"

"A surprising bonus of walking, to be sure."

"Yes, I get lots of great bonuses from walking," Marianne replied. "I've lost almost twenty pounds and I feel great. Not too long ago, a friend and I decided to train together to walk a half marathon—thirteen point one miles. That definitely upped my game in terms of physical activity. Plus, we really kept each other going, and it's great to have someone to talk with for all those miles. I've now done two half marathons, and the elation at the end of those finish lines is something I'll never forget.

"I walk almost every day, usually around four miles or so. On weekends, I try to do more, but if I'm not preparing for a marathon, I'm not a fanatic about how much or how often—it's more about how I feel. I really regret it, both physically and mentally, if a day goes by that I don't exercise in some fashion.

"Plus, I'm a bit of a clotheshorse—even when it comes to workout clothes. Before, I would never have dreamed of even looking at spandex, let alone wearing it, but now I really enjoy shopping for athletic clothes because I feel like I actually belong there. I own five pairs of running shoes and care about wicking fabric! Just a couple of years ago I would never have believed in such a possibility.

"In addition to walking, I've taken up other forms of exercise. A year ago I joined a nearby gym, where I work out with weights. I've got muscles for the first time in my life!

"A local sports shoe store is sponsoring a running club, and I signed up. My friends still can't believe it. *'You?'* they ask, incredulously. Like I said, I was the least likely candidate to become athletic. It amazes my friends, and I must say, it sometimes amazes me as well. I'll be sixty next year and here I am—a jock!"

"What advice would you give to others who want to become athletic, regardless of age?" I asked.

Marianne thought about it for a moment and then replied, "Connect to something you really like. For me, it's the solitude of my early morning walks. It might be something different for other people.

"Don't take on anything that in your heart of hearts you know you won't like. If you don't really like it, you'll stop doing it. So pick something that gives you pleasure.

"Weave exercise into your life. Make it pleasurable, not just one more thing on your to-do list. And try to stay away from 'shoulds' in terms of how much, how often, how fast, and so on. Be kind to yourself. You want the activity to be a joy, not a burden.

"In my experience, one thing led to another. It was a succession of little steps. The short walks led to longer walks; the long walks led to half marathons. Then I wanted to work with the rest of my body, not just my legs, so I joined the gym. And now I'm ready to move from walking to running. You build momentum as you go—it becomes easier and more fun.

"This transformation from sedentary office worker to midlife jock has given me a completely new sense of self. I love how I feel—physically, mentally, emotionally, and spiritually. It's never too late to start moving your body. If a former couch potato like me can do it, anyone can."

I always turn to the sports pages first,
which record people's
accomplishments. The front page
has nothing but man's failures.

—*Chief Justice Earl Warren,*
Supreme Court Justice

FAMOUSLY NEVER-TOO-LATE

BEAUTY, BRAINS, AND BRAWN

Geena Davis, the actress who became famous with her roles in *Thelma and Louise*, *The Fly*, and *Beetlejuice*, is not exactly a person who comes to mind when one thinks of top-ranked athletes. But a top athlete she is.

Originally, the statuesque six-foot-tall actress took up archery for recreation. Over time, her passion for the sport grew, as did her ability. In 1999, at the age of 43, she competed as a semifinalist in trials for the US Olympic Archery Team—hoping to make the team for the 2000 Olympics in Atlanta. She didn't make the team, but that didn't deter her involvement in sports.

Today, Geena is the front woman for the Women's Sports Foundation, and focuses her time and energy on equality in sports opportunities for girls and women.

And lest you think that this woman is just another pretty face with a gorgeous, fit body, you should know that Geena is also a member of American Mensa—an intellectual society whose members have IQs of 140 or higher, in the statistical top 2 percent of smart people.

What an amazing combination Geena has going for her—beauty, brains, *and* brawn!

MUTUAL FITNESS
IN THEIR 80S

Ramah and Joe are an amazing couple. Ramah is 81, Joe is 86, and they work out at the gym five days a week! I asked them to tell me their story.

"I was athletic when I was a boy," Joe began. "Growing up in Bombay, India (where I was born a British subject), I was into all the sports of that time—squash, tennis, water polo, rugby, and the rest. But then I joined the army in 1940 and all my sports activities stopped.

"I got out of the army in 1946 and took my first job as an earthmoving engineer, reclaiming land. I did that for a couple of years, then went to work for Gulf Oil, where I worked for the next thirty years, first as a lubrication engineer and later as a marketing coordinator. I put all my energy into my career during those years and didn't have much time for athletics. As a result, by the time I retired in 1986, my weight was up to a hundred ninety or a hundred ninety-five. I didn't like that at all. I was five feet nine inches tall, and that's too much weight for someone my height."

"What did you do about it?" I asked.

"I joined a local gym, hired a trainer for a few sessions, and then continued on my own," Joe replied. "That was over twenty years ago, and I still get up at five A.M. every morning and go to the gym with Ramah."

I turned my attention to his wife. "Is your story similar to Joe's?"

"Yes and no," Ramah replied. "I was born in Calcutta in the nineteen-twenties, and girls back then were not supposed to be athletic. There were no sports like there were for the boys. So I grew up doing more sedentary, feminine things such as homemaking, reading, the arts, fashion, and beauty.

"Joe and I met and married in 1954 and moved to the United States in 1966. We lived in Beverly Hills, where I worked as a beauty operator. I had been trained by Vidal Sassoon and had owned my own salon when we lived in India, so I just kept doing the same kind of work when we came to California.

"I walked to work every day, so that was one form of exercise I got on a daily basis. And I always did my own housecleaning as well—I kept an immaculate house, and that requires a lot of physical work, too. I used to joke that I didn't use a chair all day, until dinnertime. That was the first time I sat down!

"I was a beautician for seven years but finally got tired of doing hair, so when a friend told me about Drucker's in Beverly Hills, I went there to check it out. I became a manicurist and we had wonderful celebrity clients—it was very exciting and glamorous. But doing nails meant that I was sitting all day rather than being on my feet all day, so I was getting less exercise on the job than I had when I was a hair stylist."

"When did you start going to the gym?"

"I continued to work for about five years after Joe retired," Ramah replied. "He was going to the gym every day, but I could only go on weekends. But you do what you can, and working out on the weekends was better than not working out at all. When I finally retired from Drucker's in 1991, I began going to the gym with Joe five days a week."

"You two are such an inspiration," I said. "What advice would you give others who want to become more athletic, but feel that they don't have the time?"

Joe was quick to reply. "You have to make time. If you're interested in being healthy and fit, you'll make time for it. When something is important to you, you can always make time."

"We just love the way we feel after we exercise," Ramah added. "One of the things that motivates us is that we enjoy how we feel on the days we work out. We can tell the difference—if we miss a day at the gym, we're both tired at the end of the day; on the days we work out, we have plenty of energy to go out in the evenings. If you want more energy, getting vigorous exercise will do it for you."

"There's the social aspect, too," Joe chimed in. "We go every morning at the same time—we get up at five A.M. and we're at the gym by six-fifteen, like clockwork. We see the same people there all the time. We get to know each other; we develop friendships. We've made some wonderful friends over the past twenty years that we've been going to the gym. So if you want to make new friends who will help motivate you in your desire for a healthy lifestyle, going to the gym on a regular basis is a good way to do it.

"Getting exercise is not only good for your body, it's good for your mind. Getting your heart pumping and the blood circulating will clear your mind and help prevent depression. Depression is all too common among older people, and I'm convinced that if more seniors got regular exercise, their outlook and mental health would improve dramatically."

"It all sounds good to me," I said. "Anything else you'd like to add?"

Ramah and Joe thought for a moment, then Ramah replied, "I think it's been good for our marriage, too. We've been married for fifty-five years, and getting interested in getting fit has given us another way to spend time together doing something we both enjoy.

"We raised our kids together, obviously, but once the kids are grown and gone, couples need to find additional interests in common."

"I agree," Joe added. "We enjoy each other's company; we enjoy the new friends we've made; we enjoy the extra energy; and we enjoy how we look and feel. My weight is now a healthy hundred sixty-six pounds, so it makes me feel good about myself."

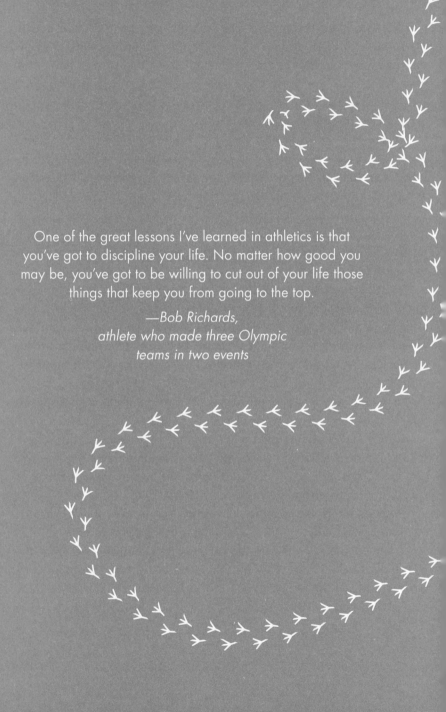

One of the great lessons I've learned in athletics is that you've got to discipline your life. No matter how good you may be, you've got to be willing to cut out of your life those things that keep you from going to the top.

—*Bob Richards,*
athlete who made three Olympic
teams in two events

NEVER-TOO-LATE TIPS FOR BECOMING ATHLETIC:

1.
Pick activities that you enjoy, so you'll be more likely to keep at it over the long haul. If you like it, you'll do it. If you don't, you won't.

2.
Start small. Set yourself up to succeed. It takes time to build new habits, so don't try to become physically fit all at once.

3.
Get an exercise buddy or personal trainer. You're more likely to show up for your athletic activities if you know someone is waiting for you.

4.
Ask your family and friends for their support and encouragement. You need all the help you can get to keep on your new fitness path.

5.
Be safe and sensible in your newfound athletic life. Warm up. Stretch. Keep yourself hydrated. Get enough rest. Listen to your body. Seek medical attention if trouble arises.

CHAPTER 7

IT'S NEVER TOO LATE TO FIND TRUE LOVE

The truth is that there is only one terminal dignity—love. And the story of a love is not important—what is important is that one is capable of love. It is perhaps the only glimpse we are permitted of eternity.

—Helen Hayes, Academy Award-winning actress

I have heard it said that a woman over 40 has a better chance of being kidnapped by a terrorist than she does of finding a husband. I don't buy it.

I've seen too many examples of older couples finding true love.

My parents, Ken and Gloria Gallagher, divorced in their 50s, after 31 years of marriage. They each moved on, found new loves, and have now been with their respective partners for 30-plus years.

My friend Joan Hill met the love of her life, Joe Donlan, when she was 60 and he a few years younger. They've been together and deeply in love for 18 years.

My friend Anita Goldstein met Paul Schneider when she was 52. She'd been married with two sons, divorced after 25 years. She met Paul in 1982 and they've been together ever since.

My mentor and dear friend Warren Bennis married a beautiful, smart woman he had been in love with 30 years earlier—when he was a young MIT professor, she a young resident at Harvard Medical School. In the intervening years, they had each married and divorced a couple of times, and raised their kids. When they reunited in 1992, it was the kind of fairy-tale happy ending you sob through in the movies. I asked Warren what it was like to finally marry Grace Gabe after all those years. He replied, "It's like coming home."

So I don't buy what those pundits say about terrorists versus late life love. I believe it's never too late to find true love. I believe it because I see it—and I see it because I believe it.

GETTING REAL

Pat McHenry Sullivan knew that she wasn't in the most ideal situation to find the man of her dreams—she was almost 40 years old, living in Washington, DC, a city in which straight single women are said to outnumber straight single men by a ratio of four to one. But Pat had discovered through years of therapy and personal growth that demographics and chronology were not the biggest barriers to finding love. Now she was insightful enough to understand that it was her own internal beliefs that were her real problem. "I had learned that you have to deal with the underlying stuff if you want to make change in your life," Pat explains. "So I realized that I was going to have to find my internal 'no' to relationships if I was ever going to have my right husband."

"Where did that 'no' come from?" I asked her.

"It developed very early in my life," she answered. "My mother was a very beautiful woman who died when I was just thirteen. As the oldest child, I had to take on her responsibilities, including caring for my younger siblings. Our father worked full-time and then some. Although my mother had taught me well to cook, make jam, can tomatoes, sew, and help run the house, I was unprepared to step into her shoes. I was haunted by the feeling *Boy, I don't measure up*. It wasn't just that I wasn't beautiful like her, but there was no way I could measure up to the idealized saintly image I gave her after she died. That feeling of not measuring up colored every aspect of my life, especially my romantic relationships."

"Well, you've been happily married for twenty-five years now, so obviously something changed in you," I commented. "Can you tell me what happened?"

"I went to a nine-day spiritual retreat sponsored by the International Pathwork Foundation—that was the turning point. It was an intensive process, conducted with a small group of people, each of them pursuing spiritual, emotional, psychological transformation.

"During the retreat, I admitted how much I just wanted a man on my arm to make me look good. I wanted a 'Henry'—someone to go places with, a guy who would enhance my self-image, make me feel complete. It was important that this 'Henry' looked good, so that I would look good.

"The group played along in a sort of psychodrama process. The facilitator told me to pick a man in the group and tell him how to be my perfect Henry. I did and he played his role to the hilt. But something weird happened—as my Henry played his role with me, I started to feel sick. Somehow, Henry didn't make me happy as I thought he would.

"You see, we all play these unconscious games in our lives. Pathwork brings your unconscious to your consciousness. It's not comfortable or fun, but it's essential if you want to get at the hidden barriers to the life you say you want.

"After Henry and I had been role-playing for a while, another man in the group suddenly spoke up. 'Do you really want a Henry or do you want a *real* relationship?' he asked me.

"I was startled, but he had my attention. 'I'm a real man looking for a real woman,' he told me. 'But right now, you turn me off because you're being phony. If you want to turn me on, you have to be real.'"

Pat went on, "This is the kind of thing women always *say* they want—but on a deeper level, we really don't. To be authentic and have an intimate relationship with another person who is also authentic is terrifying. It makes us vulnerable. I could feel the tightness in my whole body as this man spoke to me.

"Then suddenly I had a breakthrough. 'I don't want a Henry,' I blurted out, 'I want a real man.'

"I came out of that nine-day retreat knowing that I would have a real relationship—or I would be fine not having it. You know what I mean? I was willing to really go for what I wanted, but I wasn't attached to the outcome. And I was no longer looking for a Henry."

"That's pretty powerful," I said, reflecting on Pat's experience.

"Yes, it was. But that's what it took to get rid of the internal fears that were holding me back. My old baseline was: *I'll never measure up. I need a man to complete me.* And my new baseline was: *From who I am, I attract the right man.*"

"And then what happened?"

"The details aren't really important," she replied. "An interesting doctor showed up in my life. He proposed on the second date, but I wished him well and sent him on his way. Then another man showed up—a Henry. I knew right away that he wasn't the one.

"And then I met John, who was a visitor to a singles group I belonged to, Discovery on the Hill. He was quiet, almost shy, but I was immediately struck by his sense of humor, his integrity, and the way I just lit up when I was with him.

"The next week, I had a date with a wonderful man—a date that had been set up before I met John. We had a great time, but afterward I tried to connect him with other single friends, because I already knew John was my man.

"That was twenty-seven years ago—John and I have been married for the last twenty-five. He is a real man and I have become a real woman, so it worked."

"And you've lived happily ever after?"

She laughed. "Yes, but happy doesn't mean there haven't been struggles, challenges, and difficult times together. John and I love each other very much and we've weathered some really hard times—deaths in both our families, career changes for each of us, and conflict that sometimes seemed like it would do us in. So 'happily ever after' doesn't mean that bad things never happen—it means we do everything we can to take good care of ourselves, each other, and our marriage."

I asked Pat what advice she would give others who seek to find true love, at any age. She had four suggestions:

1. Be true to yourself—that's where you meet people from.
2. Have at least two or three people in your life who know who the real you is. These are the people who will help you see the goodness in yourself and will call you on your own bullsh•t.
3. Don't assume anything. Sweep away expectations. Be fully present in each and every moment, with each and every person. Practice the presence of God as you relate to other people.
4. Laugh a lot. If possible, choose in-laws who laugh a lot, too.

Pat McHenry Sullivan and her husband John Sullivan are cofounders of the Spirit and Work Resource Center (www.spiritandworkresourcecenter.com).
Pat is the author of many articles and two books on how to work with increased integrity, purpose, and joy.

Maybe love is like luck. You have
to go all the way to find it.

—Robert Mitchum, actor

Love is not finding someone to live with—it's finding
someone you can't live without.

—Rafael Ortiz, boxer

IT'S NEVER TOO LATE TO
LOVE...

LISTEN with unconditional acceptance.
OPEN your heart to the joy—and the pain.
VOICE your feelings.
EMBRACE every opportunity to love.

Time is too slow for those who wait, too swift for those who
fear, too long for those who grieve, too short for those who
rejoice, but for those who love, time is eternity.

—*Henry van Dyke, author, educator, clergyman*

FOOTWORK AND TIMING

Diane Spatz has led an amazing life. She worked for years as a senior editor for one of the top newspapers in the country, working on exciting political stories, going to many of the A-list parties, and rubbing shoulders with politicos, wonks, pundits, and kingmakers. It was a fabulous life for a single gal. Then she met Mr. Wonderful and stepped off the career ladder to enjoy a whole new lifestyle of golf, skiing, building a dream house, and hanging around with the country club set. Diane went from writing the news to just reading it—and she's never looked back.

"I guess the best place to begin my story is 1987, when I gave up dating," Diane said. "I was married for six years in my twenties, and had a few long-term relationships after my divorce. I dated off and on over the years, including a living-together arrangement. In 1987 I met a guy through work and began what I thought was going to be a great long-term relationship, but it wasn't. He wasn't ready, or wasn't clear on what he wanted, and when we broke up, something sort of snapped in my head. *I'm done,* I decided. *I've been dating a long time now and I'm tired. It's just not worth the emotional effort anymore.*

"I was perfectly happy being alone. I had a very demanding job that kept me at the office for ten to twelve hours most days, and I came home at night just exhausted. I was pushing forty and really didn't have the mental energy for dating anymore. So I gave up men."

"How long did that last?" I asked.

"About four years," Diane replied. "I would date on the rare occasion, but I was not in the market for a long-term relationship. Then my mother died in June of 1991. That August, something clicked in my head again. *I don't want to be married to my career.* So I decided to get back in the game. I told my friends; I told my hairdresser; I put the word out that I was interested in meeting new men. I even joined one of those expensive, upscale dating services. My friends fixed me up on a few blind dates; I met some interesting men on the dating service; and people introduced me to eligible bachelors."

"It sounds as if you approached it as if you were looking for a job."

"Yes, I suppose you could say so," Diane responded. "It was a priority so I put time and energy into it accordingly. Just like a job."

"How and when did Mr. Right show up?"

"I met Bob on a blind date," Diane answered. "We were both at the point where we wanted to find a life partner—we weren't dating just for the sake of dating. We were each looking for someone we could get serious about.

"We talked on the phone a lot before we decided to meet in person. Then we agreed to meet at a local restaurant. I got there a couple of minutes early and told the hostess that I was waiting for someone. She seated me and I waited for Bob to come. Time passed—fifteen minutes, thirty minutes, forty-five minutes—and he didn't show up, so I decided to go ahead and order something to eat. I figured something must have happened to delay him.

"What I didn't know was that Bob had arrived just a few minutes after I did, but he talked to a different hostess, who then seated him at a table. So all this time, we were both there, waiting for each other! Finally, Bob decided to get up and walk around the restaurant, and that's how he found me. We both had a good laugh."

"You weren't upset while you were waiting?"

"No. Neither one of us was angry. We each thought that something had happened to the other, some kind of delay. This was in the days before cell phones, so we didn't have any easy way to call each other. Because neither of us became overwrought and put a negative connotation on the situation, it was a good beginning. That was November of 1991."

"Was it love at first sight?"

"No. Interestingly enough, on the surface, neither of us was what the other was looking for. I was a career woman with a very demanding job and Bob was retired—he was looking for a partner he could travel with. And from my perspective, a former fighter pilot and retired brokerage owner wasn't exactly the kind of guy I imagined for myself."

"When did that change?"

"I knew fairly soon," Diane said. "We were still dating other people, but by February or March I knew Bob was the man I loved. At that point, I stopped seeing other guys. But it took Bob a few more months to decide that I was the one for him. He had been badly burned in a short-lived second marriage and that made him a little gun-shy.

"He also had concerns about my career and about kids. Bob is fifteen years older than I am, with grown children and grandchildren from his first marriage. He didn't want any more kids but he was concerned that I might, even though I was in my early forties. It took a while for him to be convinced that I meant it when I said that having children wasn't important to me. And it was the same with my career—he didn't want me to feel pressured to give up my wonderful career, only to resent him later.

"It took about four years for us to work through all those issues. We broke up a couple of times and then got back together. I moved in with him once, only to move out a few months later. I always knew that I loved Bob and that he was the guy for me, but he needed more time to be sure. And he was very patient with me, too. He waited until I decided to leave my job and join him in full-time retirement. So there was a willingness on both sides to work out potential problems that could have ultimately destroyed the relationship."

"One of the things I've heard you say, Diane, is, 'Love is holding someone close, with your arms open wide.' Can you say more about that?"

"Well, I think it's a mistake to cling to someone because you love him so much or you're afraid he'll leave," Diane explained. "Holding too tight actually makes the other person feel trapped and want to escape. When you get to our age, both people need to come to the relationship willingly, not because they have to be together. There were no kids or financial needs to bind us together. It was important that each of us chose to be together simply because we wanted to."

"It takes a lot of emotional maturity to do that, don't you think?"

"All I know is that if one person isn't ready, the other needs to allow time and space to let his or her partner be sure. The timing must be right for both people. You can't force it; you can't rush it. If you do, it'll backfire.

"We finally got engaged in 1994 and I moved in for good. It was wonderful. We had no big need to get married so we just stayed engaged. Finally, in 2003 we married. We were a bit anxious about getting married—we were afraid things would change. They did—for the better!

"Some of the things that make it work for us: We both come from the Midwest so we share common values. We're very good friends and love being together, talking, or just hanging out. Sometimes in the morning we sit in bed for hours, sipping cokes and talking. We don't always agree, but that's okay. We don't have to agree on everything—sometimes we agree to disagree.

"Bob is good for me because he pushes me in directions I wouldn't go on my own—he's got me doing all sorts of outdoor things like skiing, golf, whitewater rafting, and all that. Without him I'd probably just be curled up with a good book all day. And I'm good for him, too. We complement each other." Diane smiled. "And it doesn't hurt that he's good-looking."

"What advice would you give other people who want to find true love?"

"First, I think you need to be really clear on what you want,"

Diane replied. "I had my famous 'Three S Test' when I was dating: Single, Straight, and Solvent."

I chuckled. "That's pretty funny."

"That was just the first cut," Diane said with a laugh. "You'd be surprised how hard that was to find in the dating world!

"But, seriously, I wanted a man who was smart, confident in himself, and fun to be with. I needed someone who wasn't threatened by my high-powered job or the money I made. Bob wasn't intimidated or bothered in the least. And he liked the fact that I didn't need him for his money. Many men fear that women are just looking for a successful man to be their meal ticket.

"Second, you have to put the word out that you're looking for a mate. You have to go places, be social, put yourself into places where you're likely to meet appropriate men. You have no idea how many Smithsonian Museum singles lectures/cocktail parties I attended, among other events. Tell your friends what you want; enlist others in finding good candidates for you to choose from.

"Third, you have to work at it. Some people say that love falls into your lap when you least expect it—that hasn't been my experience. I made a commitment to finding love. I prefer a steady relationship to dating lots of new people, so the dating process was not that much fun for me—it took enormous mental energy. I realized that I probably would have to meet and date several men before I found the right man.

"But it paid off—Bob and I found each other. All these years later, we still love being together."

Love is the greatest refreshment in life.
—*Pablo Picasso, artist*

BOY MEETS GIRL.
BOY GETS GIRL.

There's something in the human mind that loves a happy ending. Deep down inside we all want to feel good, and reading books or watching movies with happy endings reassures us that all is right with the world. No matter how many challenges the characters face, we love it when they manage to work things out in the end.

It's understandable, then, that actors Tom Poston and Suzanne Pleshette brought smiles to millions of people when they married in May 2001. Poston was 79 and Pleshette was 64. The two had first met 42 years earlier, in 1959, when they costarred in the Broadway comedy *Golden Fleecing*. They became a hot item at the time, but their love affair ultimately soured.

Each moved on to marry other people in 1968—Pleshette married businessman Tom Gallagher and Poston married homemaker Kay Hudson.

The two actors worked together again on *The Bob Newhart Show* in the '70s—Pleshette played the role of Newhart's wife and Poston guest-starred as Newhart's college buddy. But Pleshette still nursed hard feelings against her ex-beau, so much so that she frequently encouraged Newhart to dump Poston from the show. "I didn't like him," Pleshette later confessed. "I kept telling Bob, 'Get rid of him.'"

Fast-forward to summer of 2000, when the two actors, both grieving over the deaths of their longtime spouses, reconnected again. Grief must have softened Pleshette's heart; the two became friends. Soon the friendship blossomed into love. "We commiserated with each other and ended up being married, and I'm as happy as I've ever been," Poston said in July 2002 (quoted in "Late Bloomers" by Ed Bark for Back Channels).

People magazine reported that Tom "proposed in time-honored fashion, to Pleshette's alarm. 'When he got on his knee,' she said, 'I thought he fell, and I tried to pick him up.'" (*People* magazine, May 28, 2001.)

Ooh, I just love those happy endings. Tears of laughter, tears of joy—somebody hand me a hankie, please.

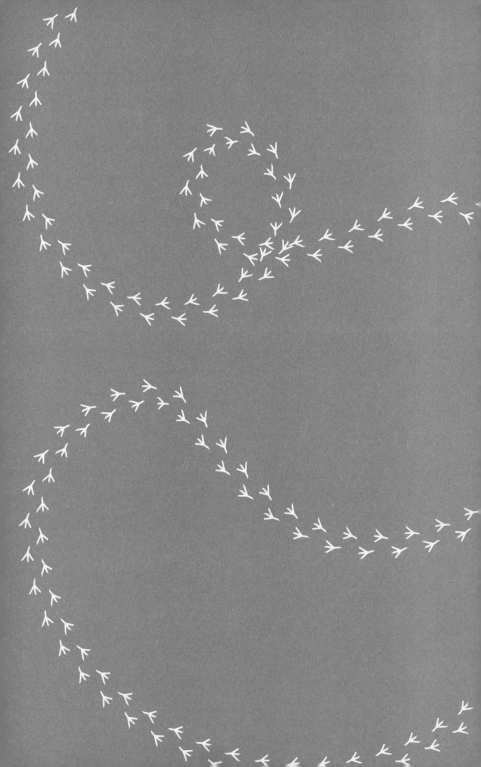

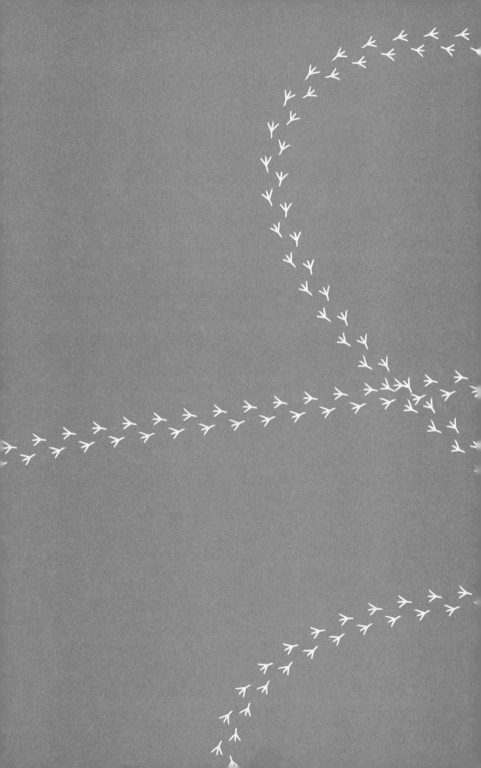

SOUL WORK TO FIND
A SOUL MATE

Many people say that love is better the second time around. Oakland trial lawyer Gary Gwilliam would certainly agree.

"The year 1990 was one of internal struggle, change, and transformation," Gary began his story. "I was fifty-two years old and working hard to lose weight and get fit, both physically and mentally. I was very active in my law firm, with a heavy caseload. But mostly, I was looking for answers."

"What kind of answers?" I asked him.

"Answers to those big existential questions," Gary replied. "You know, the kind that most people ask at some point in their lives. The questioning and searching often comes in midlife—it did for me. *Who am I? What is my life purpose? How can I be happy?* That's what was on my mind. Foremost among these questions was: *What shall I do about my marriage?*"

"Your marriage? What was wrong with your marriage?"

"My wife, Liz, and I have been together for twenty years, married for nineteen. We'd had such a wonderful relationship in our early years in the seventies, but later on, our marriage suffered due to my heavy drinking and frequent infidelities, combined with intense work stress.

"I finally quit drinking for good in 1986, with the help of a support group for lawyers called The Other Bar. But giving up booze was the easy part—the harder part was the journey of self-development upon which I embarked. I was working with psychics, engaged in hypnotherapy, and seeing past-life therapists. I was willing to go anywhere and everywhere to see people I thought might help me in coming to terms with the Big Issues of my life.

"I had already been divorced once, and I was determined to make a go of this second marriage. Liz and I had two wonderful kids, ages fifteen and seventeen. We had a big, beautiful four-bedroom house in the hills of Oakland, with a second home on the beach near Monterey. We even had the perfect family dog, a dachshund named Sam. On the outside, our life looked perfect.

"But inside, it was another story. Liz and I bickered frequently. She was depressed and irritable. I was under enormous stress at work. We would lose our tempers over the silliest things sometimes—but the fights were serious and our relationship was getting harder and harder. We both acknowledged how difficult it was to hang in there, but we were committed to doing everything we could to make it work."

"It sounds pretty grim."

"It was," Gary said. "Grim and bleak."

"Sounds like a marriage of gritted teeth."

Gary nodded. "Yes. Liz and I both knew that sooner or later, something had to give. We were going to have either a breakthrough or a breakup."

"So which was it?"

"In April of 1990 I went to a New Age and metaphysical expo in San Francisco. I saw a woman who advertised intuitive readings for fifteen dollars. Her name was Dr. Susan Stuart. Something attracted me to her, so I approached and asked for a reading. I told her I wanted to talk about relationships. She asked if there was someone special I wanted to discuss, and I said, 'Yes. Her name is Liz.' The psychic sat back, closed her eyes, and went into a meditative state for a few minutes. Then she wrote 'Liz' in cursive in the air with her finger. She then opened her eyes, looked at me, and said, 'That relationship is over.'

"Intuitively I knew she was right, but I wasn't ready to accept it. I told her I wanted to schedule another session to get a more detailed reading. I did that the next month. The psychic reiterated what she had told me about Liz and then said something even more important. She told me I was going to meet someone new before the end of the year. I wasn't even ready to leave Liz yet, and this psychic was telling me a new romance was on the horizon!"

"That's really something."

"No kidding," Gary concurred. "As a general rule, I do not accept predictions from psychics. If their information is valuable, intuitive, and makes sense, then I listen to it. If not, I reject it. I'm a lawyer. I think logically and rationally. I don't accept stuff unless it seems rational. But something about Susan's comments seemed so profound—her words rang true for me."

"Did you walk away from your marriage, then?"

"No," Gary replied. "I wasn't ready to throw in the towel. Liz and I spent the next few months trying our best to salvage our marriage. She went to therapy and I read books about relationships. We took a trip to Spain, which was wonderful. But as soon as we returned home, the problems started again.

"It finally came to a head in September when we went to a weekend workshop with a man named Lee Coit. It was a group session in which we had to deal very honestly with our feelings. I think by the end of the weekend we had both come to the same conclusion. We knew we really loved each other but the passion was gone. Our marriage was over and it was time for us to move on.

"Perhaps my journal entry will best describe what happened next:

I told Liz I was going to move out on Wednesday evening. She was very upset that night and into the next day. However, when I came home from work the next day, something dramatic had happened. She had changed. She said she had accepted the decision and knew it was right for both of us. I felt like I was listening to a new woman. She then told me that after our conversation she had sat quietly in the bedroom that morning in tears and frustration and had the most amazing spiri-

tual experience of her life. She was in tears and asked God for help. Then a light came over her and she felt at peace for almost the first time in her life. She knew herself that it was time for us to leave, that our separation was the right thing. It was the best conversation we had had in over fifteen years. For my part, I felt a huge load lifted from me and I am now ready for some freedom."

"That's a very powerful story," I murmured.

"Yes," Gary said. "Liz's spiritual experience gave me the answer I had been looking for. I wanted to leave Liz with integrity. We both had to be right with it, for ourselves, and especially for our children. I was determined that our separation would be done with mutual love, integrity, and compassion.

"I moved into a little apartment and the grieving began. Divorce is like death, and I was filled with pain and sadness. I missed my dog; I missed my home; I missed my children most of all. But I had to make it on my own. I had to accept whatever happened. I felt that all my hard work over the years was coming to fruition. I was grateful to be sober and wasn't tempted to return to drinking. I felt the universe was going to bring me what I needed, what I had asked for—a soul mate, a truly spiritual relationship. But there was no predicting when or if it would come."

"Waiting is the hard part, isn't it?"

"Yes, it is," Gary replied. "Like most people, I'm always eager for what's next, particularly if it's something positive. But I'm not in charge of the universe, so I have to be patient and trust."

"Did you have to wait long?"

"Not very. In early November, I attended a meeting of California trial lawyers in La Jolla. It was a meeting I attended every year, but this time I was alone. I had to explain to my friends and colleagues that Liz and I had separated. I felt strange, somehow distant from the couples and friends I had known for so many years. It was painful, grieving the loss of my marriage.

"One evening, my friend Ed, who had helped me quit drinking, invited me to attend an AA meeting. I don't usually attend AA meetings, but the trial lawyers were holding a special, late-night candlelight meeting for those in recovery. When it was my turn to tell my story, I shared about my drinking years, how my friends and family had staged an intervention, and what my life was like now that I was sober. And of course, I shared about my separation from Liz, and how it had come about.

"After the meeting, a woman came up to me and said, 'I just want to tell you that I really appreciate your integrity. So many men leave their marriage for another woman. You left because you knew it was the right thing. I left my own marriage the same way a number of years ago. I really wish you the best and simply wanted to say that.'

"I appreciated her comments, but I thought she was dating one of the other guys who was in the meeting, so I really didn't think much more about it. But a few days later she called me at my office. She told me later that her intuition had told her to pick up the phone, despite the fact that she knew I was an alcoholic and a two-time loser—Liz was my second divorce. She had had a strong intuitive feeling that she should call me, and despite misgivings, she followed her feelings. She told me her name was Lilly. She was not an alchoholic; she'd been at the AA meeting to support her friend. We had a lovely phone conversation and made plans to meet over Thanksgiving weekend when she came to the Bay Area to visit her daughter.

"Lilly drove up from Los Angeles a couple of weeks later and we met as planned at my little apartment in Oakland. She had a couple of glasses of wine and I had my nonalcoholic wine. We started to talk, and I have to tell you, it was the most amazing, open discussion that I had ever had with a woman. I decided that I was going to be completely honest and tell Lilly nothing but the truth. This was a new me: total honesty.

"We went out for a lovely dinner and then went back to my apartment to talk some more. I put on a little slow music and we danced. I enjoyed our conversation and was attracted to Lilly, but it wasn't about sex. I just felt really comfortable with her—amazing, since this was only our first date.

"After dancing for a few minutes, I heard a voice in my head—a voice I'll never forget. It said, 'This is her.' I couldn't believe it. *What was that?* Then the voice said again, 'This is her.' Immediately I had an incredible vision of Lilly and me living a life together—traveling all over the world and having the most wonderful relationship I could ever imagine. That vision lasted only a few seconds—it was like a flash. I didn't know what to think. *Was it my imagination? Was it God? Was it Susan Stuart's prediction coming true?* Whatever it was, it was powerful.

"Lilly and I had only known each other for about three hours, so what came out of my mouth next must have sounded really weird to her: 'I'm in love with you and we're going to spend the rest of our lives together.' She looked at me but didn't respond. I wondered if she felt the same way, or if she thought I was crazy. But somehow or other, I think she knew the same thing. She smiled as she said simply, 'Who knows?'

"Lilly had had several glasses of wine, so I encouraged her not to drive to her daughter's house. I explained that my apartment had two bedrooms and she could have her choice—either a small pullout bed in the second bedroom or the waterbed in my much larger master bedroom. I guess the choice was easy. But strangely, the evening wasn't about sex; it was just that we felt completely comfortable with each other. We climbed into bed and I read to her from *Journey of the Heart: The Path of Conscious Love*, by John Welwood, a book I had been reading recently.

"The next morning, we were still talking about why we had this incredible sense of companionship, of already knowing each other, and of being so connected. We decided to get a past-life reading from a hypnotherapist I'd seen a few times. Her name was Kay Weatherly and fortunately she had time to see us that very morning.

"Over the course of three readings in that session, Kay told us that Lilly and I had lived together as brother and sister in eighteenth-century Europe. We had a long and loving life as siblings, totally platonic. In the second reading Kay said that we had also been father and daughter in a previous life. I have three daughters in this life, so the notion of Lilly as my daughter helped explain the feeling of closeness, especially on this Thanksgiving holiday weekend. In the third reading, Kay said that Lilly and I had known each other in ancient Egypt, but our genders had been reversed—Lilly had been a temple high priest and I had been a married worshipper in the temple. But the priest, Lilly, seduced me and we had a wild, passionate affair.

"After the readings, we left in a bit of a daze. It seemed like we'd always known each other, and yet we hadn't even had a full twenty-four hours together on this, our first day. Suddenly, I broke into laughter—it all seemed so funny and I couldn't stop laughing. 'What's wrong?' Lilly asked. 'I don't know,' I replied. 'This is the funniest damn thing. I don't know whether I'm your brother or your father. I don't know whether you're a man or a woman. I don't know what the hell is going on but you look great to me. Let's go back to the apartment and make love.'

"So we did. She stayed another night, which was absolutely wonderful. We were in love. It seemed like we had always been in love; we felt so connected. It wasn't like anything I've ever felt before or since, at least not in this life. That was eighteen years ago, and we've been together ever since."

"That's an amazing story," I said. "What advice would you give others who aspire to find true love in their own lives?"

"A couple of things," Gary said. "First, true love is not for the young. I think you have to know who you are and what your life is about first. I wasn't ready for a real relationship until I had experienced a lot of life, read a lot of books, delved into personal development work and therapy, and really come to understand myself. By then I was fifty-three—Lilly was forty-eight. Whether you're seeking a new relationship or starting an old relationship over again, self-knowledge is essential.

"Second, the purpose of a spiritual relationship, any good relationship, is not to make you happy. Many people feel that making each other happy is all there is. But I think happiness is a by-product of spiritual growth. I can't make somebody else happy and she can't make me happy. We can do things that *contribute* to happiness, but happiness comes from within.

"The purpose is to grow together so each of you can become the best human being you can be. The relationship serves that purpose, which is the same purpose of life. Here's how I often describe it: Think of two candles burning brightly next to each other as you hold one in each hand. Now, slowly bring the candles together at the tips and watch the two flames join each other. They become one larger, brighter flame. That describes Lilly and me—that describes what happens when two souls come together in true love. Both become better, brighter."

For more information about Gary Gwilliam, his books, his speaking availability, and his law practice, visit www.giccb.com/bio/GaryGwilliam.asp.

It's never too late to fall in love.
—Sandy Wilson, author

NEVER-TOO-LATE TIPS FOR FINDING TRUE LOVE

1.
Get clarity about the kind of partner who would be right for you. Write a list of the five most important characteristics of your perfect partner. Create a mental picture of this ideal person.

2.
Understand that your perfect partner might show up in unexpected ways. He or she may not look exactly like what you had imagined. Take time to look below the surface. Don't make snap judgments.

3.
Put yourself in social situations and places, doing things you enjoy. You want to meet someone with common interests, so stay busy doing things you love.

4.
Flirt—often.

5.
Tap into spiritual resources as part of your quest for true love.

CONCLUSION

"That which is the most personal is also the most universal," a wise editor once told me. His words echoed in my head as I gathered stories for this book. He was so right. Deep down inside, we all want the same things: acceptance of who we are as individuals, acknowledgement and appreciation, love and companionship, opportunities to grow, fulfillment in our work, financial security, and the possibility of living our dreams. We all want to be our best selves—in our personal, as well as professional, lives.

In writing this book, I can now tell you that I had a personal agenda—I did it as much for myself as for you. Here's the back story...

I have a Big Birthday coming up this year—you know, one of those birthdays with a zero in it. One morning not too long ago, I was putting on my makeup and noticed many laugh lines in my face. I frowned. Sigh.

Well, I guess it's too late, the voice of my old companion, Hopelessness, whispered in my mind. *You're getting older and you still haven't met the right guy. You've been single quite a while now, since your divorce. You're not going to remarry. It's too late.*

But Hopeless didn't stop there: *Face it, sweetheart, you've made mistakes along the way—in your career, in handling money, in not taking better care of your body. Now it's too late. You'll never lose weight; you'll never get into shape. Nor will you achieve the level of success you desire.*

Sadness rolled over me like a blanket of fog rolling over the hills of San Francisco, obliterating the view. Heavy sigh. I stared glumly at my reflection in the bathroom mirror.

Later that day I was doing some reading and came across a quote from George Eliot: "It's never too late to become what you might have been."

My morose fog layer instantly started to lift. I repeated the words to myself in the mirror—again and again, like an actor rehearsing an important line. "It's never too late to become what you might have been," I pronounced with emphasis.

Then I said, "Go away!" to Hopelessness, who still wanted to hang around. "I'm not going to listen to you anymore," I scolded. "You're just plain wrong."

Hopelessness fell silent.

"From now on, my new mantra is: It's never too late to become what you might have been," I announced to the mirror. So what if there's a Big Birthday coming up? I've still got lots of birthdays and lots of life left.

That was six months ago. Hopelessness still comes around once in a while, like an old lover who was never any good for me. Sometimes he catches me off-guard and I find myself beginning to listen to his doubt and despair. But it doesn't last long. When I catch myself falling under his spell, I shoo him away again with my new mantra.

So you see, writing this book was a labor of love—for you, my dear readers, and for myself. This book is my line in the sand. I'm now stepping over it into a new chapter in my life.

I'm delighted that you, too, are staking out your own future, undeterred by voices of doubt and insecurity. For what George Eliot said is true—it's never too late to become what we might have been.

ABOUT THE AUTHOR

BJ GALLAGHER is an inspirational author and speaker. She writes business books that educate and empower, women's books that enlighten and entertain, and gift books that inspire and inform. Whether her audience is corporate suits, working women, or the general public, her message is powerful, positive, and practical. She motivates and teaches with empathy, understanding, and more than a little humor.

BJ's international best seller *A Peacock in the Land of Penguins* (Berrett-Koehler, third edition, 2001) has sold over 300,000 copies in 22 languages. Her other books include *Everything I Need to Know I Learned from Other Women* (Conari, 2002) and *YES Lives in the Land of NO* (Berrett-Koehler, 2006).

BJ and her books have been featured on *The CBS Evening News* with Bob Schieffer, *The Today Show* with Matt Lauer, Fox News, PBS, CNN, and other television and radio programs. She is quoted almost weekly in various newspapers, women's magazines, and websites, including *O: The Oprah Magazine*, *Redbook*, *Woman's World*, *Ladies' Home Journal*, *First for Women*, the *New York Times*, the *Chicago Tribune*, the *Wall Street Journal*, the *Christian Science Monitor*, the *Orlando Sentinel*, the *Seattle Post-Intelligencer*, CareerBuilder.com, MSNBC.com, ClubMom.com, and SavvyMiss.com, among others.

In addition to writing books, BJ also conducts seminars and delivers keynote addresses at conferences and professional meetings across the country. Her corporate clients include IBM, Chevron, John Deere, Credit Canada, Volkswagen, Farm Credit Services of America, Raytheon, Marathon Realty (Canada), Chrysler, Atlanta Journal-Constitution, Phoenix Newspapers Inc., Infiniti, and Nissan, among others.

She has taught public seminars on Leadership Skills for Women in Mexico and Colombia. Here in the US, she works regularly with chapter presidents and members of the National Assistance League.

BJ is the former manager of training and development for the Los Angeles Times, where she was responsible for management development, sales training, customer service seminars, diversity training, specialized programs for women, and the development of high-potential managers.

BJ is a Phi Beta Kappa graduate of the University of Southern California, earning summa cum laude honors with her BA in Sociology. She has completed the coursework for a PhD in Social Ethics, also at USC.

For more about BJ Gallagher and her books,
visit www.womenneed2know.com
or www.peacockproductions.com.